A WINNING DIALECT

A Winning Dialect

Reinventing Linguistic Tradition in Rural Norway

THEA R. STRAND

TC TEACHING CULTURE

UNIVERSITY OF TORONTO PRESS
Toronto Buffalo London

Toronto Buffalo London
utorontopress.com
Printed in the USA

ISBN 978-1-4875-4595-6 (cloth)
ISBN 978-1-4875-4596-3 (paper)
ISBN 978-1-4875-4597-0 (EPUB)
ISBN 978-1-4875-4598-7 (PDF)

Library and Archives Canada Cataloguing in Publication

Title: A winning dialect : reinventing linguistic tradition in rural Norway / Thea R. Strand.
Names: Strand, Thea R., author.
Series: Teaching culture.
Description: Series statement: Teaching culture : UTP ethnographies for the classroom | Includes bibliographical references and index.
Identifiers: Canadiana (print) 2023062216X | Canadiana (ebook) 20230622283 | ISBN 9781487545956 (cloth) | ISBN 9781487545963 (paper) | ISBN 9781487545987 (PDF) | ISBN 9781487545970 (EPUB)
Subjects: LCSH: Norwegian language – Dialects – Norway – Valdres. | LCSH: Language and culture – Norway – Valdres. | LCSH: Valdres (Norway) – Economic conditions. | LCSH: Norway – Rural conditions.
Classification: LCC PD2698.V35 S77 2024 | DDC 439.8/279481 – dc23

Cover design: Liz Harasymczuk
Cover image: Wikimedia Commons / Øyvind Holmstad

We welcome comments and suggestions regarding any aspect of our publications – please feel free to contact us at news@utorontopress.com or visit us at utorontopress.com.

Every effort has been made to contact copyright holders; in the event of an error or omission, please notify the publisher.

We wish to acknowledge the land on which the University of Toronto Press operates. This land is the traditional territory of the Wendat, the Anishnaabeg, the Haudenosaunee, the Métis, and the Mississaugas of the Credit First Nation.

University of Toronto Press acknowledges the financial support of the Government of Canada and the Ontario Arts Council, an agency of the Government of Ontario, for its publishing activities.

Funded by the Government of Canada | Financé par le gouvernement du Canada

Contents

Illustrations

Figures

Tables

Preface and Acknowledgments

I have spent most of my fifteen years as a professional anthropologist teaching, and I have taught mostly undergraduate students in introductory and intermediate cultural and linguistic anthropology classes. With those students and classes in mind, I have tried to write this book in a clear, concise, and accessible manner, and I hope that it may serve as a useful and compelling case study in linguistic anthropology, including for students with no previous experience in anthropology or linguistics. As an ethnography, this book documents the complex social and cultural life of language in Valdres, a rural district in central Norway with a distinctive and popular local dialect. The book's central themes, around which its five core chapters are organized, include language ideologies and hierarchies, language planning and standardization, linguistic stereotypes and style, motivations for language change, and the commodification of language and culture, all of which have been critical strands of linguistic-anthropological research over the last several decades. My intention is that students and instructors will find the book useful not just for learning about the particularities of language and dialect in Valdres and in Norway, but also for learning and teaching a wide variety of core concepts in contemporary linguistic anthropology. Additionally, I hope that it may be used to explore some of those key topics in greater depth and comparative perspective at more advanced levels of study and that it will be an informative contribution to the ethnographic study of contemporary Europe and of rural communities.

I also expect that this book will have readers with a particular interest in Norway, Valdres, regional dialects, or all of those things at once, and I am mindful that it is somewhat different from many other accounts of language and dialect in Norway. Research in Norwegian sociolinguistics, which encompasses ethnographic approaches like this one, has most often been undertaken by scholars who are native speakers raised in Norway and trained specifically in Norwegian linguistics. This book is different in many ways, as I was raised in the United States and did not learn to read and write in Norwegian until my teenage years. As a child, I first learned Norwegian in its spoken form from my father at home and extended family in Valdres, then partly forgot it, but living and working in Valdres after college greatly strengthened my latent Norwegian skills. I have come to know the district and its dialect intimately, and I am as enamored of them as anyone. But I grew up in the United States with English as my dominant language, so my perspective on language in Valdres and Norway is inescapably that of an insider-outsider, as we are sometimes called in anthropology. I understand local viewpoints thoroughly, but I also sometimes interpret things somewhat differently because of my American background, as well as my anthropological training, making this book a rather unusual contribution to the study of dialect in Norway. It is the case that all accounts are partial, but I hope my unavoidable insider-outsiderness is not too much of an irritation for Norwegian readers, especially those in Valdres who participated in and contributed their time and energy to this research, for which I am incredibly grateful.

Central Valdres is a small place, where it often seems that everyone knows everyone, and I use pseudonyms to protect the privacy of the people who graciously sat with me for interviews and other conversations, entertained my endless questions, and generously offered up their wisdom and words, along with copious amounts of coffee and cake. They know who they are, and I am deeply appreciative of each of their contributions. My research in Valdres was also aided immensely by my relatives there, especially Turid Kj. Berge, Eivind Strand, Ola Berge, Ragnhild Strand, and Gro Berge, who helped me with all manner of practical things as I navigated living, working, and doing research in Valdres early on.

I am also grateful to my parents, Connie Hilberg Strand and Morten Strand, who cultivated ancestral connections to Norway throughout my childhood, including many visits to see family in Valdres, without which I would have been ill-equipped to undertake this research, much less build the career I have. Thank you for all of those things and so much more.

Much of the research and some of the writing for this book were begun when I was a graduate student learning from an incredible group of mentors and doctoral committee members, including Jane Hill, Susan Philips, Norma Mendoza-Denton, and Malcah Yaeger-Dror. From them I received invaluable training, wisdom, and early feedback on my initial attempts at ethnographic and sociolinguistic research.

Some of the writing and examples in this book have been previously published in Strand (2012a, 2012b, 2015, 2019). I thank the editors and reviewers of those articles and chapters for their thoughtful feedback, with special gratitude to Misty Jaffe and Sabina Perrino among them. I am also grateful for constructive comments and questions received at conference presentations of data and ideas throughout the book from 2005 to 2018, including American Anthropological Association (AAA) annual meetings, Sociolinguistics Symposium, and International Conference on Language Variation in Europe events, among others. I especially thank Jillian Cavanaugh, who served as discussant for AAA panels in which I participated in 2010 and 2018 and provided substantive and encouraging comments on work in progress that has now finally made its way into print.

I sincerely appreciate the thoughtful feedback provided by series editor John Barker and the several anonymous reviewers of the proposal and manuscript for this book, as well as the support from my editor at UTP, Carli Hansen. My wonderful colleague Ruth Gomberg-Muñoz also provided incisive comments on chapter drafts, for which I am grateful. I also owe thanks to my colleagues Kristin Krueger and Catherine Nichols, as well as to my faculty writing group, for their support during the writing process.

The biggest thank you goes to my closest collaborator in work and in life, Michael Wroblewski. This book could not have come to fruition without his contributions of patience, intellectual inspiration, and in-house editorial support. His humor and love, and that of our daughters, Elsa and Clara, are a sustaining force.

Work on this project from 2007 to 2012 was supported with grant and fellowship funding from the Wenner-Gren Foundation, the American-Scandinavian Foundation, the American Association of University Women, the University of Arizona Department of Anthropology, and the University of Massachusetts Amherst College of Social and Behavioral Sciences.

CHAPTER ONE

Winning the Dialect Popularity Contest

Sitting at their vinyl-covered kitchen table, drinking coffee and chatting with my uncle and aunt one day in June 2005, I turned my head as my ears perked up. We had just finished the morning barn chores together, feeding and tending the young calves, milking the cows, and letting them back out to graze for the day. A national radio station was on in the background, as it always was, and the morning show hosts were encouraging listeners to call in and vote for their favorite Norwegian dialect. My uncle noticed, too, and, knowing that I was studying anthropology and linguistics, he was pleased to tell me that the Valdres dialect, *our* dialect, was on the list of nominees for the radio contest. It was not entirely surprising to us that Valdres made the list. We knew it was a beautiful place, both in the farm-dotted, deep "home" valleys and in the mountains, where locals took their cattle and sheep to graze in the summer and tourists had been flocking for prime hiking and cross-country skiing opportunities for the last century. But the local dialect, with its unique words and unusual pronunciations, had not always been appreciated outside of Valdres. Hearing that it was among the leading candidates for Norway's most popular dialect left us in eager anticipation of the contest's outcome.

As a budding linguistic anthropologist, I was also very curious to observe which dialects made the list, how they were winnowed out over the course of the summer, and what being in the running would mean for language and cultural life in Valdres, a district that had been struggling with a downturn in traditional family farming due to rising costs of living in Norway and the globalization of food markets. As it turned out, the Valdres dialect ended up winning the contest, and it became a point of both pride and some contention within the valley as a result, revealing generational divides in definitions and perceptions of dialect. Additionally, and just as importantly, the contest shed light on dominant Norwegian beliefs about language in general, rural dialects in particular, and what those things have to do with Norwegian history, culture, and identity.

The status of regional dialects in Norway is clearly different from most Western nations, where relatively strong notions of "standard" and "correct" speech often contribute to marginalization and stigma around regional dialects or accents. Having a strong Southern or New York accent in the US, for example, can be a liability, especially when interacting with Americans from more "standard"-sounding places. In Europe, similar cases abound; in France, for example, Parisian French has had prestige and authority throughout the country, while France's regional ways of speaking have been dismissed as unintelligible "patois," largely excluded from formal and institutional settings and historically even targeted for eradication. As elsewhere (including in the English-speaking world), "proper" ways of speaking and writing the French language, and even what has counted as "language" at all, have been those most closely associated with political and economic elites in the capital. This kind of sociolinguistic system is exceedingly common – and may even feel commonsense to those who have grown up within it. But language and dialect in contemporary Norway are different, offering an alternative model in which traditional regional ways of speaking are highly valued and enjoy widespread popular support.

This book tells the story of how one regional Norwegian dialect, called *Valdresmål* or *Vallers*, has been transformed in recent decades, changing both linguistically and culturally as it has been put to new uses in the twenty-first century. As life-long residents have had to adapt to changing social, economic, and political circumstances – particularly the shift from family farming to tourism development – they have used local linguistic and cultural resources, including their dialect, to craft a viable future for themselves and the places their ancestors have called home for centuries. Once stigmatized as poor and uneducated, today the distinctive dialect of Valdres holds a special place as a marker of local belonging and also as a valuable part of Norwegian national heritage, both of which were on full display in the radio show dialect popularity contest and its aftermath.

THE *REISERADIOEN* CONTEST

The first-of-its-kind dialect contest was held on Norway's most listened-to national radio network, NRK P1, as part of its popular summer morning variety show, called *Reiseradioen* (Travel Radio). With an average daily audience of nearly 750,000 listeners that summer (in a country of less than five million people), *Reiseradioen* beat its next two radio program competitors combined. The program featured live broadcasts focused on summer activities and human-interest stories from throughout Norway, running from mid-June to mid-August. A typical daily show included reports or interviews from a coastal sailing town, a mountain hiking destination, or a campground at the edge of an inland fjord, as well as frequent weather and water-temperature reports, trivia quizzes, lost-and-found notices from listeners, and call-in greetings to friends and family during summer vacation, a time when many Norwegians retreat to mountain or seaside cabins, which, before smartphones, usually lacked television and internet but almost always had a radio.

The *Reiseradioen* dialect popularity contest came at the peak of reality programming in Norway and in the midst of a broader trend in radio and television toward audience participation via phone or text message. The contest was interactive, and listeners were first encouraged to nominate their favorite Norwegian dialects, then prompted to vote on progressively shorter lists, as each week ended with *Idol*-esque eliminations of those receiving the fewest votes.

In Norway, as in many other national contexts, geographic dialects (*dialekter*) are representative of specific places, whether regional or local, and dialects differ from one another in pronunciation, grammar, and vocabulary, so that people from different parts of the country often speak Norwegian differently. Despite these differences, there is enough mutual intelligibility across dialects that people can still usually understand one another without too much trouble – similar to, say, English as spoken in Appalachia versus California in the United States. Linguists often quip that "a language is a dialect with an army and a navy," pointing out that (1) the boundaries between "languages" and "dialects" are blurry and not solely based on mutual (un)intelligibility but more often on political borders, and that (2) the ways of speaking and writing that are usually described as "languages" (and *not* dialects) originate among elites and have the power and authority of nation-states behind them. What *dialect* means is thus a complex issue for anthropologists and linguists, but the notion of "dialect" as a traditional, regional way of speaking is at once taken for granted and hard to escape in Norway, where cities, towns, and rural areas around the country have named dialects associated with them.

In the early days of the *Reiseradioen* contest, Norwegians' awareness of and interest in the country's many dialects were on full display: the initial list of nominated dialects numbered over 200, as the hosts reported on-air, and it contained dialects from all four of Norway's popularly recognized dialect regions: East, West, South, and North. While these regions do not necessarily correspond to those identified by professional linguists, they do represent what sociolinguist Dennis Preston (1989) has called a dominant "folk dialectology." Early on, the nominees included both urban and rural dialects, some of which were fairly specific – the dialect of a particular city, for instance – and others that were much broader, naming the dialect of an entire *fylke*, the geographic and political equivalent of a smallish US state. As the contest progressed, however, more and more of the Northern, Southern, and urban dialects failed to receive enough votes to move on to the next week's round and were eliminated.

The top ten dialects that remained in the third-to-last round included rural dialects from both Eastern and Western Norway, as well as the distinctive and often-parodied dialects of the country's second- and third-largest cities, Bergen and Trondheim. Oslo, Norway's capital and largest city, was conspicuously absent, reflecting national beliefs about language that conceptualize urban Oslo as something of a dialect void. This underscores how ways of speaking that count as "dialect" often stand in contrast to what is perceived as standard or normative "language," even though, of course, there are plenty of linguistic forms and features that originate in and are characteristic of the capital city. But Oslo's historically high status and political centrality have allowed its speech patterns to sound "normal" and not like a dialect at all, making it an unsuitable candidate for the *Reiseradioen* contest.

Prior to the final two rounds of voting, then, the contest included a variety of candidates that were generally representative of Norway's dialectal diversity. Leading the top-ten list, however, were four dialects that belonged to a single linguistic region: Vest-Telemark, Hallingdal, Nord-Gudbrandsdal, and Valdres are all located in what Norwegian linguists refer to as the *Midlandsk* (Central) dialect area. As its name suggests, the Midlandsk region is located roughly in the middle of the country, along the eastern edge of the mountainous divide that separates the coastal fjords of Western Norway from the inland valleys and forests of Eastern Norway. While the Midlandsk region belongs geographically to Eastern Norway (*Østlandet*), Midlandsk dialects differ from *Østlandsk* (Eastern) dialects as a result of centuries of trade and social and linguistic contact with Western Norway.

The last two rounds of the *Reiseradioen* contest – first an elimination among the top three dialects and then a showdown between the final two – featured exclusively rural dialects from the Midlandsk region. And the winner voted Norway's Most Popular Dialect was … Valdres, a mostly agricultural valley in East-central Norway that is also nationally well-known for the spectacular mountain landscapes bordering the district on three sides. The Valdres dialect, also called *Valdresmål* or, more colloquially, *Vallers*, had led the contest each week in the second half of the summer and received nearly 60 percent of the votes in the final round, leading to much local celebration and debate.

Over the course of the entire summer that year, the dialect contest was a nearly unavoidable source of entertainment and suspense for hundreds of thousands of Norwegians, including many people I knew in Valdres, who participated by calling or texting in their votes, and even for those who simply followed along without voting. The contest was reported on in television newscasts and in local and national newspapers on a weekly basis and generated countless op-ed pieces. But how could a dialect popularity contest become such a successful pop culture phenomenon in the first place? Why would the dialect of a rural farming valley with a population of just 18,000 come out on top? And what effects might the contest have for Valdres and Valdresmål? It turns out that a good place to start in answering these questions is Norwegian mass media, where the country's notoriously complicated sociolinguistic situation and ideologies of language are regularly on display.

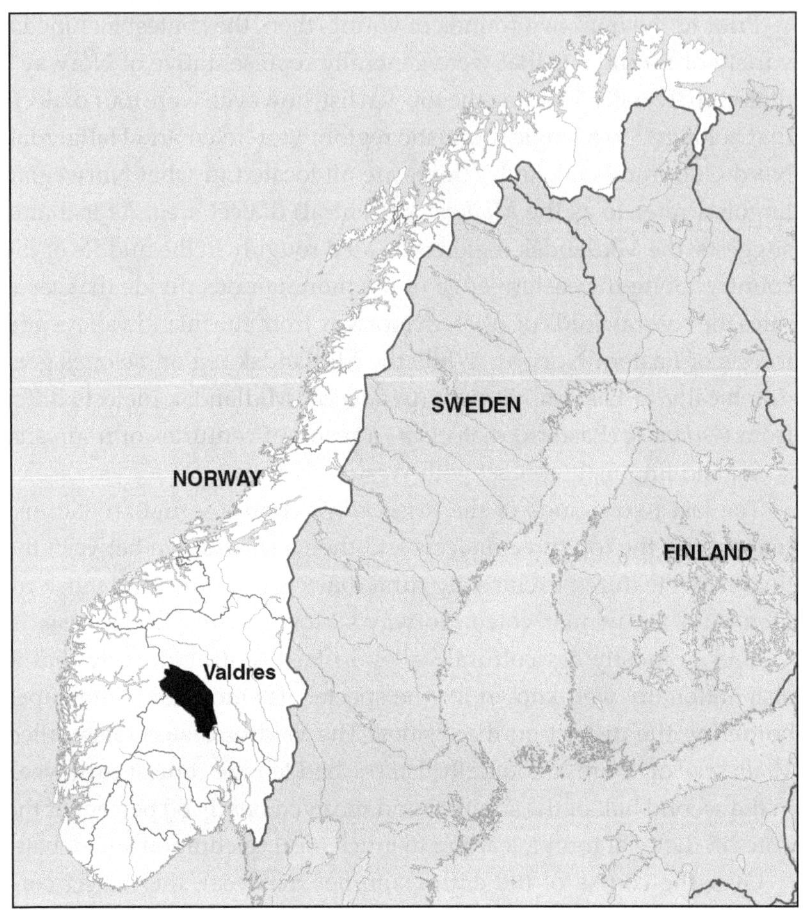

Figure 1.1. Map of Norway showing the location of Valdres. Adapted from NordNordWest, CC BY-SA 3.0.

DOMINANT IDEOLOGIES OF LANGUAGE IN NORWAY

The idea of a national dialect contest might have been new with the 2005 season of *Reiseradioen*, but the general popularity of programming about language in Norwegian media was not. The *Reiseradioen* contest came along just a year after the debut of the award-winning and wildly successful *Typisk Norsk* (Typical(ly) Norwegian), a national primetime television series focused on the Norwegian language in both its written and spoken forms. *Typisk Norsk* included features highlighting the social aspects of language, stories about significant events in the history of Norwegian all the way back to Old Norse, and even celebrity guests, who were subjected to pop quizzes about language in general and Norwegian in particular. The program also included a regular bit called "Guess the Dialect," in which a brief video of a Norwegian dialect speaker was played, and viewers could win a prize for correctly guessing the speaker's hometown or district. In the early 2000s, the weekly national radio programs *Språkteigen* (The Linguistic Sign) and *Språkspalten* (The Language Column) also presented popular audiences with lay-level facts about language and grammar, as well as recent research on Norwegian, including interviews with academic linguists. They also provided tips and advice on "good" language use, often in response to listener-submitted questions. While less popular than *Typisk Norsk*, these programs have nevertheless enjoyed long lifetimes, with *Språkteigen* on the air since 1974 and now available as a podcast, attesting to what Norwegian-American linguist Einar Haugen observed half a century ago as an unusually high level of general interest in language in Norway (Haugen 1972). This is so much the case that the topic of language also pops up frequently in general programming, as it did in the *Reiseradioen* dialect contest.

In the Norwegian context, all of this points to popular linguistic awareness, as well as the ways in which media discourse is thoroughly saturated with *language ideologies* (Irvine 1989; Woolard and Schieffelin 1994). Following linguistic anthropologist Judith Irvine, we can understand language ideologies as "the cultural system of ideas about social and linguistic relationships, together with their loading of moral and political interests" (1989, 255). Taken as a whole, ideas about the relationships among language, culture, and society represented in Norwegian mass media point to national language ideologies that positively value distinctive local and regional dialects and dialect use.

Looking beyond programming *about* language and dialects, we can also see these language ideologies reflected in the great many Norwegian newscasts, sportscasts, debates, game shows, reality shows, and other television and radio programs that are frequently broadcast *in dialect*. Which is to say that people on Norwegian television and radio often speak in their own native, non-normative dialects, even when "reading" the news or other scripted material, and program guests and contestants are (and feel) free to use their own dialects, as well. Essentially, there is no national "broadcast standard," like one might expect to hear on NBC or CNN in the US, for example, and, according to official statistics for NRK (the Norwegian equivalent of the UK's BBC), the average percentage of national programming broadcast in dialect in Norway was about 38 percent for radio and 24 percent for television during the first decade of the twenty-first century (Statistikk Sentralbyrå 2009).

In this sense, implicit language ideologies valuing dialect use and linguistic diversity are continuously reproduced through the regular use of local and regional dialects in Norwegian media, which is an important part of how, according to Debra Spitulnik Vidali, mass media play a key role in shaping widespread beliefs about language, "as [media] give value to certain language codes, linguistic varieties, and discourse styles" (Spitulnik 1999, 149). Both in the amount of programming focused on language and in the regular use of non-normative speech varieties, Norwegian broadcast media can thus be viewed as a significant site for the production and reproduction of dominant language ideologies valuing the country's distinctive spoken dialects. As linguistic anthropologist Asif Agha has argued regarding the decline of conservative RP in British media, where producers consciously moved away from elite speech forms, "once such choices are made, patterns of exemplification in the mass media themselves amplify the processes of which they are a part" (Agha 2007, 225).

In the Norwegian case, we also see mass media capitalizing on language-focused programs, reflecting a popular, everyday interest in sociolinguistic variation and dialectology there since at least the middle of the twentieth century. Haugen (1966, 1972) described the situation in Norway as one of linguistic "hyperawareness" resulting from several generations of intense political debate over the standardization of written Norwegian, which will be discussed in much greater detail in Chapter 2. For now, suffice it to say that the history of the current sociolinguistic situation in Norway is indeed complex and tied to more than a century of highly politicized language planning and struggle (Haugen 1966; Bucken-Knapp 2003; Jahr 2014).

Since becoming a fully independent nation-state in 1905, Norway has had two legally equal written norms, *Bokmål* and *Nynorsk*, which involve a considerable amount of variation, both across the two and within each of them. The use of Bokmål and Nynorsk is regulated in print and broadcast media, in official government communications, and in education. In the private sector, Norwegians may freely choose between Bokmål and Nynorsk, but reading and writing in Bokmål is preferred by a significant majority. The Bokmål written norm was originally based on Danish and is a relic of Denmark's control of Norway from the Middle Ages until 1814, while the Nynorsk written norm was originally based on a survey of spoken rural dialects undertaken by the linguist Ivar Aasen in the middle of the nineteenth century, following the end of Danish rule. Bokmål is therefore associated with Oslo, Norway's cosmopolitan capital and former center of Danish administration. In contrast, written Nynorsk is understood to represent the distinctive spoken dialects of outlying rural areas, both linguistically and symbolically.

Perhaps more important for understanding the 2005 dialect popularity contest, however, is the fact that there is no official or authoritative standard for *spoken* Norwegian (Sandøy 2009), and Norwegians are encouraged to use their native dialects when speaking, even in relatively formal contexts, like politics, education, and mass media. Observing this as something of a peculiarity within Europe, Jahr and Janicki (1995) have noted that "Norwegians use local dialects more often and to a much larger degree than other European nations. Dialect use is seen as normal linguistic behavior" (30). Still, despite the general acceptability and appreciation of regional dialects today, the forms of Norwegian spoken in urban Eastern Norway, especially Oslo, function as a de facto national (or, at least, regional) spoken norm (Mæhlum 2009; Røyneland 2009; Mæhlum and Røyneland 2018), in the sense that they are perceived as "normal" or "unmarked." That is, they are not popularly understood to be geographic dialects in the same way as "marked," or non-normative, local and regional ways of speaking. This sociolinguistic fact is closely linked to the historic political and economic dominance of Oslo and other Eastern cities. However, following the discovery of vast oil reserves in Norwegian territory in the 1960s, the national economy and politics have been reconfigured, and resources have been more equitably distributed. Today, state and popular commitments to social and political equality underlie policies like universal healthcare and welfare, but they also support sociolinguistic diversity and a widely shared sense of the value of local linguistic and cultural traditions. Among other places, we can see this in contemporary mass media, where marked dialects have a strong presence, especially compared to their relative absence there just fifty years ago. Taking the historic and contemporary sociolinguistic situations into consideration, the logic and appeal of the *Reiseradioen* dialect contest make good cultural sense. But why did Valdres, among Norway's many distinct dialects and locales, come out on top? What makes the district and its dialect special, and how do Valdresmål speakers perceive their distinctive ways of speaking and the contest win?

NORWAY'S MOST POPULAR DIALECT

Valdres is a large inland valley located near the center of Norway's southern lobe. While it is part of Eastern Norway (*Østlandet*) by virtue of its location on the eastern side of the country's north-south-running mountains, Valdres lies in the westernmost part of Eastern Norway and thus belongs to the Midlandsk dialect region, as mentioned above. With just under 18,000 permanent residents occupying an area slightly larger than the US state of Delaware, Valdres is a rural agricultural district with small-scale dairy farming and timber extraction as its long-standing economic base. At the same time, Valdres also has some of Norway's most spectacular and idyllic mountain areas, which locals have historically used for summer livestock grazing but which today attract an ever-increasing number of recreational tourists, who are often charmed by intermingling with cows and sheep while hiking and biking among the low-mountain *støler* (summer farms).

For me, the central part of the Valdres valley is also where my father was born and raised in the 1950s–1970s, and it was home to most of his (and half of my) ancestors for several centuries. Our last name, Strand, was taken from a place that has long been the site of a group of family farms, an unusually flat stretch on the shore (*strand*) of a long, deep lake called *Strandefjorden*, or *Strøndafjorden* in proper Valdresmål, which cuts through the heart of the Valdres valley. Growing up in a small town in the US Midwest, I learned Norwegian as it was spoken to me by my father and by my relatives in Valdres, whom we often visited during the summer. Spending time on my aunts' and uncles' farms was the

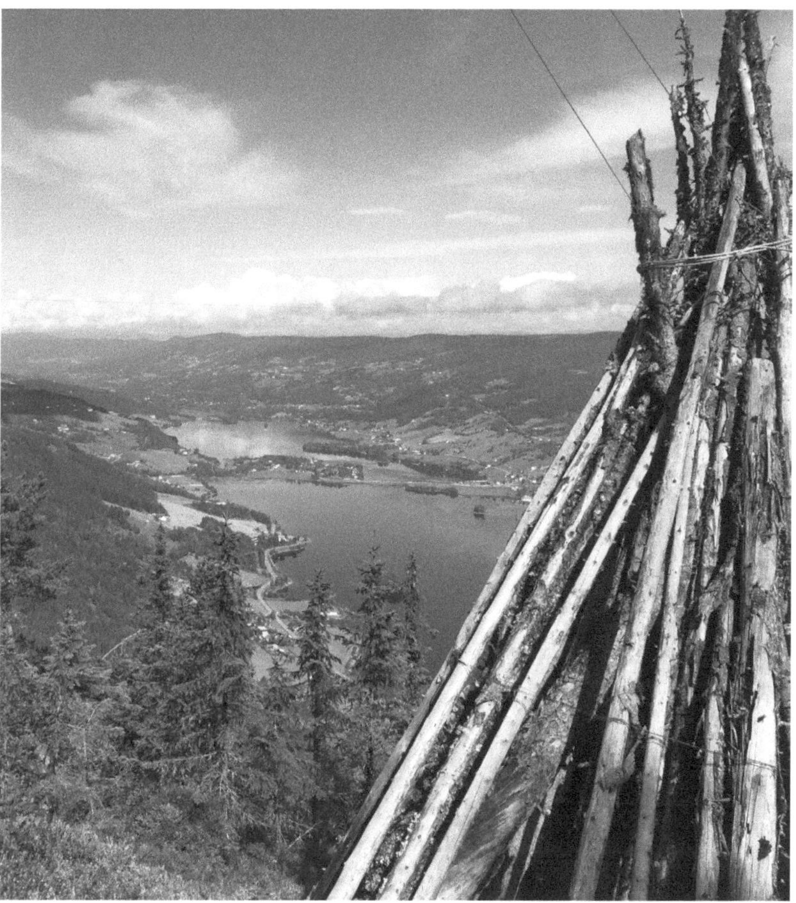

Figure 1.2. The central Valdres valley.

highlight of those childhood visits for me, and it was how I first developed a strong connection to the people and places of Valdres. I have many fond memories of observing and participating in what were, to me at the time, immensely entertaining goings-on in their dairy barns, hay fields, *støler*, and always-bustling homes, where my much-older cousins and an eclectic group of farm hands filtered in and out. That early, informal participant-observation, along with a rather bewildering experience in a Norwegian language class in high school – where I learned that I did not, in fact, speak "Norwegian" but instead a rather unusual dialect – eventually led me to undergraduate and graduate training in anthropology and linguistics.

Figure 1.3. Cattle grazing along a mountain road in Valdres.

By the time I began formal ethnographic and linguistic fieldwork in Valdres in 2007, I had already lived and worked there as an elementary teacher's aide for more than a year in 2002–3 and spent several whole summers there, sometimes working as a farm hand to pay for my airfare and living expenses. My family ties, work connections, and deep familiarity with the area all fed into the kinds of questions I was interested in exploring in my early research in Valdres, as well as the kinds of interactions I had when conducting initial ethnographic interviews with dozens of Valdres residents in 2007–8. While those early interviews were only loosely structured, they focused on language use and language ideologies, and one of the items toward the bottom of the list of themes I was interested in asking about was the *Reiseradioen* dialect contest. Initially, I considered it to be somewhat tangential to my central research questions, which had to do with dialect use and language change in Valdres; however, in almost every case, my interviewees brought up the dialect contest on their own, before I had gotten that far in my list of interview topics. Questions about whether people liked their native dialect, what features they thought of as most characteristic, and whether they were comfortable using Valdresmål in Oslo or other parts of the country all frequently elicited responses involving the contest, which itself served as a source of support for arguments about Valdresmål's many positive qualities.

Early on in an interview with Stian, a high school student at the time, I asked about his opinion of the local dialect, which I had heard him use on stage in the annual high school musical that year. As shown in lines 7 and 8 below, he replied with his own rhetorical (or perhaps ironic) question, implying the absurdity of *my* question, given Valdresmål's status as the dialect contest winner. (For a complete list of transcription conventions, see Appendix A.)

(1) T: *E det noko som du har hørt heime?*
Is it [dialect] something that you've heard at home?
(2) *Bruke begge foreldro dine valdresdialekt?*
Do both of your parents use the Valdres dialect?
(3) S: *Ja, begge to bruke valdresdialekt.*
Yes, both of them use Valdres dialect.
(4) *Då e det ganske naturle å prate det sjøl med.*
So then it's pretty natural to speak it myself too.
(5) T: *Har du brukt valdresdialekt heile tie, enn e det noko so –*
Have you always used Valdres dialect, or is it something that –
(6) S: *E ha brukt den heile tie, så det.*
I've always used it, so.
(7) T: *Ko syns du om dialekta di? Liker du den?*
What do you think about your dialect? Do you like it?
(8) S: *Ja, ja. @@ E ho ikkji norges finaste dialekt?*
Yeah, yeah. @@ Isn't it Norway's nicest dialect?
(9) T: *Jo. @ Syns du det sjøl at ho e det?*
Sure. @ Do you think so yourself?
(10) S: *Ja, det synst e . . . roleg og fin.*
Yeah, I think so . . . relaxed and nice.

For Stian and many other Valdresmål speakers, the dialect contest had become a significant part of how they thought about the local dialect. Notably, however, the youngest generations (those in their teens, twenties, and thirties) seemed to take special pride in the contest win. Middle-aged and older people were also proud of speaking Norway's most popular dialect, but their overwhelmingly positive opinion of traditional Valdresmål was somewhat less affected by the outcome of the dialect contest. On the whole, there was and remains widespread agreement with nationally dominant language ideologies that value Norway's distinctive local dialects, but clear generational differences in local understandings of what constitutes Valdresmål emerged as I talked to younger, middle-aged, and older residents.

The oldest people I interviewed, born in the 1920s and 1930s, often expressed their disappointment that local youth no longer spoke the "traditional" dialect. "It's so watered down now," Marie, a Valdres native in her late sixties, told me between sips of dark black coffee and drags on her cigarette. "Kids today …" she offered as a summary complaint of shifting language and life in the valley, as we sat together in an old *sæl,* the main living quarters on her family's summer mountain farm (*støl*), perched just above a large mountain lake. It was June and sunny that day, and Marie occasionally swatted at a few flies buzzing around us at the table. But a cool breeze came off the snow that remained in the impressive mountains surrounding us. In just a couple of weeks, the area would be full of tourists there to enjoy the dramatic scenery, hiking, biking, and boating through a landscape historically used in the short Norwegian summer for open grazing of cattle, sheep, and goats and fishing for sustenance. Today, these are on the wane, increasingly viewed as cost-ineffective and otherwise incompatible with "modern" life. For Marie and many older people in Valdres, the connection between the trend away from traditional livelihoods and a perceived decline in young people's dialect use was more than obvious. Like older generations in many communities, Marie was nostalgic for the old days and saw some of the ways that young people talked and acted as a problem.

For their part, though, most of the younger Valdres residents I spoke with seemed much less concerned with dialect change, including, for example, the loss of some traditional words or the dative case grammatical system – two ongoing changes discussed in Chapter 4 that have particular salience and are widely bemoaned by their grandparents' generation. Instead, Valdres youth generally believe that they still speak "dialect," even though many have experienced being corrected or directly criticized by older generations for not always using "pure" Valdresmål. In fact, though, a critical factor in the contemporary revalorization of Valdresmål is its high status among younger speakers, many of whom agree that using dialect in Valdres today is unmistakably *tøff* (cool). I even encountered a good number of high-schoolers who described themselves to me as Bokmål speakers but told me they wished they could use dialect more because of its social value among their peers.

These varying attitudes toward the state of language and culture in Valdres also came to the surface when I asked people more directly about the dialect contest. Despite a positive view of Valdresmål and dialect use across generations, people tended to agree that winning the *Reiseradioen* contest was a real shock, or at least not something they had expected from the outset. But their reasoning on this point varied. Younger people were surprised Valdres could top some of the urban dialects in the contest with so many more speakers, or, relatedly, they said that outsiders were often quicker to recognize other, "bigger" dialects. Older Valdres residents, on the other hand, often argued that some of the other dialect contest finalists were "purer" or better maintained than Valdresmål, as Marie implied during our conversation at her *støl*:

(1) T: *Ja, så var det den dialektkåringa for nokon år sia.*
Yes, so then there was the dialect contest a few years ago.

(2) *Følde du med då den gjekk på:: [e: på radioen?*
Did you follow along when it was running on:: [um: the radio?

(3) M: *[Ja, det gjorde e.*
[Yes, I did.

(4) *Ja. O det forundra me stort at valdresdialekte kunne vinne fram.*
Yes. And it really surprised me that the Valdres dialect could win.

(5) T: *Det gjorde det, ja?*
Oh, it did?

(6) M: *Ja, det gjorde faktisk det.*
Yes, it did actually.

(7) T: *Hm . . . Ja, kofør det?*
Hm . . . And why is that?

(8) M: *Jau::, for det e:: inndrage før mykji:: . . .*
Well:: because:: [people have] pulled in too much:: . . .

(9) *ja, e veit kji um e ska seia fremmandise ord,*
I don't know if I should say foreign [i.e., strange] words,

(10) *men ikkji slek som mø uttala dei.*
but [they're] not the way we pronounce them.

(11) *Nei, så det forundra me stort.*
No, so that really surprised me.

Language ideologies that value rural dialect purity and disapprove of dialect "mixing" were also found to be prevalent decades ago among speakers in rural Northern Norway in Blom and Gumperz's classic study of codeswitching between Ranamål dialect and Bokmål (1972; see also Mæhlum 1996). Purist ideologies have been documented elsewhere, in communities around the world, but ordinarily they are focused on protecting whole languages from the intrusion of foreign loanwords or grammar from other, more powerful languages. In Valdres today, however, it is *dialect* "purity" that is at stake for some, and it appears there is an age-graded language-ideological configuration, in which the oldest speakers are most concerned about nonlocal Norwegian words and grammar being used instead of, or in combination with, distinctly local forms. This is not uncommon in rural dialect-speaking areas of Norway, as sociolinguist Unn Røyneland found similar attitudes in her research in the areas of Tynset and Røros, to the northeast of Valdres. There, she reported that "mixing standard variants into the local dialect … has traditionally particularly been held in contempt and considered unauthentic … [however,] young people today do not seem to be as negative toward mixed varieties as people used to be" (Røyneland 2009, 14). And the same is true in Valdres.

It is important to note that none of these local beliefs about dialect use or linguistic purity include assumptions about any linguistic superiority for the de facto Oslo-based speech norm, referred to in Valdres as either *bymål* (city language) or simply "Bokmål" (which is technically only a written variety). By contrast, London English or Parisian French, as spoken by the middle and upper classes, tend to be held in high regard throughout their respective countries (and well beyond, in fact). But in Valdres today, dialect speakers are often openly skeptical of Oslo speech and strongly in support of dominant language ideologies valuing distinctive, traditional dialects like their own. Gerd and Harald, two married, middle-aged Valdres residents, offered a partial explanation:

(1) G: *[I dialekt] då har du ein god del ORD som e så betegnande.*
[In dialect] you have a lot of WORDS that are so descriptive.
(2) *Som du på ein måte du ikkji har i: eit meir sånn eh: BYområde.*
That you in a way you don't have in: a more like uh: URBAN area.
(3) *[E syns det –*
[I think it –
(4) H: *[Du kan si slek som berre ordet –*
[You could say just like the word –
(5) *ordet altså for potet. Kantøffel.*
like the word for potato. Kantøffel.
(6) *I Valdres e det i alle fall FIRE begrep før det.*
In Valdres there are at least FOUR expressions for that.
(7) *O det har du ikkji i Oslo.*
And you don't have that in Oslo.
(8) T: *Nei.*
No.
(9) G: *Nei. Så det bi ei mykjy meir –*
No. So it becomes a much more –
(10) *det bli eit mykjy fla::tare språk.*
it becomes a much fla::tter language.

This sort of position was at one time counterhegemonic or oppositional, as evidenced in a radical political slogan from the 1970s imploring Norwegians to "Write Nynorsk, Speak Dialect!" But the 2005 dialect contest phenomenon is a clear signal that the conventional *linguistic marketplace* – in which social theorist Pierre Bourdieu (1991) describes "standard" language as highly valued and using a regional dialect as a serious liability – has been upended in contemporary Norway. In ethnographic interviews, elderly Valdres residents do, indeed, recall experiences of linguistic discrimination and inequality in Oslo continuing at least into the 1970s, but young people eagerly express their disregard for what urban outsiders might think about their dialect use. Bourdieu argued that "the sense of the value of one's own linguistic products is a fundamental dimension of the sense of knowing the place which one occupies in the social space" (1991, 83), and it seems there have been significant shifts in Norwegian social space in recent decades. In both everyday and mediatized metalinguistic discourse (i.e., talk about talk), we can see that the linguistic marketplace in Norway is not one of social stratification correlating with radically different (e)valuations of speech from different parts of the country. Clearly, this is not just about language but also, and always, bound up with larger social, economic, and political forces. In Norway, as Sandøy (1998) has pointed out, the shift toward a revalorization of rural dialect use from the 1980s onward coincided with regional economic upturns outside the Oslo area, including in Valdres and its presently booming tourism industry.

But if all Norwegian dialects are positively valued, and dialect use is looked upon favorably, then how could *Reiseradioen* ask listeners to choose a single dialect as Norway's most popular? Across dozens of interviews and many casual discussions, only two people I talked to saw this as problematic; both were well-educated women in their forties, and one went so far as to say that she had not voted because she perceived the aims of the contest to be divisive and inegalitarian. But most people in Valdres seemed to believe that the contest promoted a very positive view of Norwegian dialects and had no problem naming their own likes and dislikes among the country's diverse spoken varieties. Indeed, the *Reiseradioen* contest's explicit aim was to name the country's "most popular" dialect, and listeners were asked to submit and vote for their "favorite" dialects. Based on the contest's large audience participation numbers, this way of thinking about language made good sense throughout Norway.

In the aftermath of the contest win, however, very few people in Valdres remember the contest as being concerned with selecting Norway's "most popular" or "favorite" dialect. Instead, there is a nearly categorical memory of the contest selecting Valdresmål as Norway's *finaste* (nicest) dialect. This points to some sort of dialect hierarchy and suggests the existence of a broader linguistic aesthetic in Norway, one not based on the usual standard-valorizing system and not yet very well articulated in explicit metalinguistic discourse. People everywhere have linguistic preferences, though, and these typically have much more to do with history, politics, and social relations than with language per se. The preferences expressed in the *Reiseradioen* contest reveal deeper underlying beliefs about language, culture, and identity, both in Valdres and in Norway more broadly.

LINGUISTIC AESTHETICS AND CULTURAL VALUE

In her research on dialect and culture change in Bergamo in Northern Italy, anthropologist Jillian Cavanaugh (2009) describes a "social aesthetics of language" that is the "interweaving of culturally shaped and emotionally felt dimensions of language use and the extra-linguistic factors that rank people and their groups into hierarchies" (11). This is useful for thinking about the situation in Valdres, as well, where linguistic awareness and preferences are part and parcel of everyday life. The notion of linguistic aesthetics has also been explored in sociolinguistic research in perceptual dialectology, which deals with nonlinguists' assessments of geographic dialects, with particular attention to people's perceptions of things like correctness, pleasantness, and linguistic difference (Preston 1989; Niedzielski and Preston 2000). In combination, these approaches allow for a more complete understanding of the linguistic *and* sociocultural evaluations that underlie any aesthetics of language, whether at the local, regional, national, or even global level.

Given the general acceptability of non-normative dialect use across casual and formal settings in Norway, perceptions of linguistic correctness seem to be less relevant than in the United States, for example, where a great deal of perceptual dialectology research shows that regional dialects are usually regarded as "incorrect" compared to "standard" American English. Cultural ideas about pleasant language, on the other hand, are very relevant to the task of picking a favorite (or "nicest") dialect. And as I talked to people in Valdres about Valdresmål and the *Reiseradioen* contest, a social aesthetic of language emerged that might be used to define linguistic pleasantness within the Norwegian context. In their positive evaluations of the Valdres dialect, some people I talked to simply said that it was "nice" or "clear," while others described it with more ideologically and morally loaded terms, like "trustworthy" or "Ur-Norwegian."

Table 1.1 includes a list of Valdresmål's key characteristics, based on interviews from the early years following the dialect popularity contest, where I asked dozens of people something along the lines of "How would you describe the Valdres dialect?" In response, I heard absolutely no negative assessments of Valdresmål, unless we wish to count *bondsk* (farmerly); however, I believe this is, in fact, a positive or, at worst, neutral assessment in both the local and national contexts, where rurality is viewed in rather romantic terms, as part of a common Norwegian heritage. Looking at the list in Table 1.1, all but the last six items are subjective assessments of supposed qualities that also happen to fit nicely with semiotician C.S. Peirce's concept of "qualisigns," representative of "an overarching value system [based on] habits and intuitions rather than rules and cognitions" (Keane 2003, 415). As in Irvine's classic account of Wolof speech registers in Senegal (1990), the perceived qualities of a particular way of speaking are not absolute measures; rather, their meaning derives from their relationships to other elements in the larger cultural and linguistic system. And, as in Irvine's Senegalese example and Cavanaugh's Italian one, the social significance of this kind of linguistic value system has to do with its "produc[tion] at the intersection of power and emotion" (Cavanaugh 2009, 11).

This list of Valdresmål's redeeming qualities represents a particular perspective, both geographically and ideologically. It associates the perceived positive qualities of the dialect with supposed characteristics of its speakers through "iconization" (Irvine and Gal 2000), ideologically linking linguistic features – like the last six items in the list – to the kinds of people and ways of being (supposedly) found in Valdres. Given the tens of thousands of people who voted for Valdresmål in the *Reiseradioen* contest, it seems that perceptions of Valdresmål as pleasant must be fairly common outside of Valdres, as well. And it is therefore also probable that many of the positive characteristics named by Valdres residents belong to a shared set of "habits and intuitions" for perceiving and evaluating language variation that extends beyond the local district, circulated and reproduced in part through their representation in national media far beyond the 2005 dialect contest.

While we cannot know for certain who actually voted for Valdresmål, people I talked to had plenty of theories. A few told me the win could be credited almost entirely to a very strong *lokalpatriotisme* (local patriotism) among Valdres residents, many of whom voted multiple times

Table 1.1. Qualities and characteristics of Valdresmål, as reported by local residents in recorded interviews

Quality (in Norwegian)	English gloss
*fin**	nice*
*klar**	clear*
rein	pure/clear
*lett/enkel å forstå**	easy to understand*
behageleg å høyre på	pleasant to listen to
*fin klang**	nice resonance/tone*
*fin tonefall**	nice intonation contours*
*flyt**	fluidity*
*melodiøs**	melodical*
musikalsk	musical
"mø syng når mø prate"	"we sing when we talk"
ikkje brå eller hard	not abrupt or hard
*roleg**	calm/relaxed*
sakte	slow
djup	deep
*stødig**	steady/solid*
trygg	secure
gledeleg	happy
*vennleg**	friendly*
troverdig	trustworthy
*bondsk**	rural/farmer-ly*
forbindelse med det urnorske	connection to the Ur-Norwegian
*forb. med norske tradisjonar, folkemusikk**	conn. to Norw. traditions, folk music*
*sære ord**	unique words*
rare ord	strange words
*fleirtall "endingadn"**	distinctive def. plural suffixes*
*mø**	distinctive first-person plural*
ikkje skarre-R	no uvular /r/
dativ kasus	dative case

Note: Entries marked with an asterisk were offered by multiple interviewees.

in each round. (Time and money were the only real constraints here, as each vote cost the equivalent of about one US dollar and took perhaps a minute or two.) Other people I talked to argued that most Valdres residents did not actually vote themselves; instead, they claimed that the district's large population of *hyttefolk* (cabin people, i.e., recreational cabin owners and tourists) voted more frequently. Some people also suggested that out-migrated Valdres natives were responsible, and a couple resorted to old regional stereotypes to help explain the win, suggesting that residents in the neighboring, rival valley of Hallingdal were too cheap (*gjerrige*) to vote repeatedly. But it was most likely a combination of local residents, cabin owners, tourists, and people with ancestral connections to Valdres who voted for Valdresmål, and Valdres's century-long history as a national tourist destination thus may have partially compensated for its small population.

Beyond perceptions of linguistic pleasantness, another measure in perceptual dialectology – degree of linguistic difference – is helpful for understanding why Valdresmål won. Both qualitative and quantitative research have shown that people tend to evaluate their own dialect and those perceived as linguistically close to their own as most pleasant; conversely, dialects perceived as very different are also often perceived as very unpleasant (e.g., Preston 1999; Fridland and Bartlett 2006; Coupland and Bishop 2007). As noted above, the Norwegian Midlandsk dialect zone, of which Valdres is a part, has historically had contact with both Eastern and Western varieties, and Midlandsk dialects share linguistic features with Eastern and Western dialect regions. Valdresmål, in particular, has had extensive historical contact with the regionally normative dialects from Oslo in the East, Bergen in the West, and the areas in between, due to its geographic position roughly halfway between these two largest Norwegian cities and location along the primary road connecting them – now highway E16, historically *Kongevegen* (The Kings' Highway), which runs straight through the Valdres valley from one end to the other. Based on what we know about correlations between pleasantness and degree of difference, people in many parts of Norway might hear Valdresmål as somewhat similar to their own dialect and find it to be relatively pleasant on that basis. This is also supported in Valdres, where people often say they like other nearby dialects, such as those of neighboring Hallingdal and Gudbrandsdal, but they tend to particularly dislike Southern dialects, with which Midlandsk dialects share the fewest salient features. For instance, as noted in Table 1.1, Valdresmål does not have a uvular /r/ sound, which is a Southern and Western dialect feature sometimes mocked in Eastern Norway.

More importantly, and in ways that are quite clearly tied to history and emotion, Norwegians are also generally fascinated by dialects with many curious, "old-fashioned" features, as documented by Røyneland (2005), among others. Valdresmål happens to have a number of very distinctive linguistic forms and features that lend it a folksy, traditional-sounding quality, and people I talked to specifically mentioned things like remnants of the dative case, peculiar plural noun suffixes, and unique and strange words, including certain pronouns. People in Valdres themselves also tend to enjoy unusual dialects, like that of Inner Sogn, which is located just over the main mountain pass leading northwest out of Valdres toward Bergen, and which is nationally notorious for its distinctive, traditional features to the point that some claim it is unintelligible. Norway's most "traditional" dialects, like those of Valdres and Sogn, are consistently presented in a positive light in national media like *Typisk Norsk*, with its dialect-guessing contest and other features highlighting particularly distinctive dialects. In Valdres, "traditional" dialect words are also identified and defined in the regular "Valdres Expression of the Day" feature in the valley's local newspaper (*Avisa Valdres*), and they are a focal point of call-in contests on the local independent radio station (Valdres Radio). In fact, when they learned that I was beginning research on Valdresmål in 2007, both the newspaper and radio station asked to interview me, and I have to confess I was more than a little anxious to be quizzed on some of the most distinctive Valdresmål words on live radio. Luckily, I passed!

Throughout Norway, mass media has played a role in the development of a kind of exotic traditionalism when it comes to a national aesthetics of language. And while "traditional" dialects are now long lost to many urbanites, they remain an important part of the national imaginary and Norwegians' sense of self in Scandinavian and European contexts (Hylland Eriksen 1993). The preference for *rural* dialects in the contest also stands out, fitting well with romantic ideologies of national identity that conceptualize Norway as a rural country and Norwegians as people with a rural heritage (Hylland Eriksen 1993), even though a majority of Norwegians have lived in urban areas since the 1950s. In Norway, "traditional" rural culture is understood to be representative of the nation to the point that "national" dress, food, and, indeed, language are all seen as best articulated in local, rural settings. This is visually evident each year on the 17th of May, Norwegian Constitution Day, when Norwegians celebrate their country's independence in part by donning the national costume (*bunad*), which has a unique combination of shapes, colors, and designs in each of more than sixty historically demarcated districts throughout the country. In this sense, as with the promotion of dialect diversity, local traditions and culture are seen as part of a common national heritage. Here, we can see how a strong emotional, perhaps patriotic, dimension of sociolinguistic aesthetics and cultural value permeated the dialect contest. Even as it promoted public dialect use and dialect diversity in general, the *Reiseradioen* contest also reinforced a national linguistic aesthetic that prefers non-normative, geographically central, rural dialects over those of the country's much more densely populated, cosmopolitan, coastal cities – quite the opposite of a conventional linguistic marketplace, with a strong, centralized "standard" language form.

DIALECT CHAMPIONS

Shortly after Valdresmål was crowned Norway's most popular dialect in August 2005, a group of Valdres youth produced a large, professionally printed banner that they marched through the center of Fagernes, the valley's largest town (pop. 1,800 at the time), and then prominently displayed in the main square. In bright, bold letters in a talk bubble coming from a cow's snout, the banner stated, "*Mø slo hallingad'n!*" (We beat the Hallingdalers!) (see Figure 1.4). Not coincidentally, these three words contain some of the most unique and iconic features of Valdresmål: the use of *mø* as the first-person plural pronoun (we) and the suffixed definite plural article *–adn* (the-pl.). Throughout Norway, *mø* is also the onomatopoetic word for the sound a cow makes (like English "moo"), which is a source of much good-natured teasing toward Valdresmål speakers, especially with dairy farming as the traditional economic base; hence the multiply meaningful use of a cow on the victory banner and elsewhere on the local scene in recent years.

As it turned out, the banner had a short-lived fate. While it was a good-humored celebration of Valdres residents' pride in the dialect contest win, it also irked shoppers, tourists, and passers-through from Hallingdal, who reportedly threatened not to return. This led to the banner's removal by district administrators who were concerned not to offend visitors or risk harm to a valuable local image, particularly following the positive outcome of the dialect contest, which was widely seen as great PR for Valdres as a region and its local businesses.

The banner also irritated a number of older language and dialect enthusiasts in the valley, including long-time leaders in pro-Nynorsk and

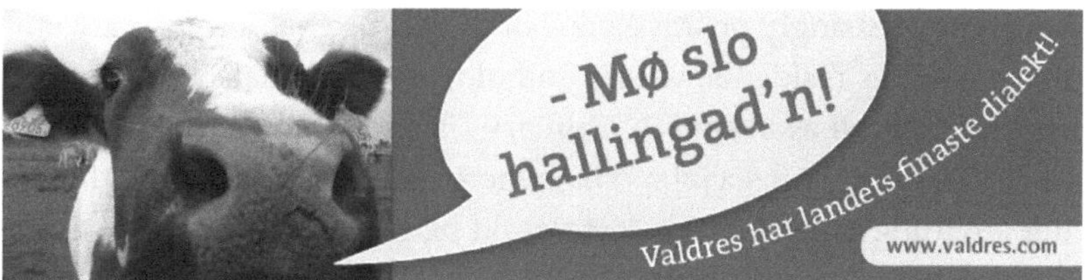

- Mø slo
hallingad'n!
Valdres har landets finaste dialekt!
www.valdres.com

Figure 1.4. Banner produced following the dialect contest win, proclaiming "'We beat the Hallingdalers!' Valdres has the country's nicest dialect!" Source: Kreativ Strek.

pro-Valdresmål activism, who reacted negatively to the use of an apostrophe in *hallingad'n* (the Hallingdalers). In interviews several years after the contest, they told me that they had been pleased to see young people using the local dialect, but they were also bothered enough by the disregard for normative Norwegian writing conventions – where apostrophes are never correct – that they could not fully support the banner. From a linguist's perspective, the use of an apostrophe shows an intuitive awareness of the syllabification of /n/ in the final consonant cluster, pronounced [ad.n̩], where /n/ is its own syllable with no intermediary vowel after /d/. And from a more anthropological perspective, this looks like one more example of a generational language-ideological divide. Generational divides over linguistic innovation are far from unique to Valdres, as older people seem to nearly universally disapprove of how young people talk and/or write (Eckert 2004). Despite a shared interest in dialect use and revalorization, many older Valdres residents continue to be very concerned with perceived impurities in contemporary Valdresmål use, while younger folks are eager to use dialect in innovative ways, including writing a historically mostly-spoken variety and sometimes doing so rather cheekily, with no permission from local authorities, linguistic or otherwise.

The creative and strategic use of the local dialect in public and in print on the banner was not the only evidence of a renewed sense of pride in Valdresmål following the contest win. According to a former leader of the local Nynorsk organization, which also supports spoken dialect use as part of its mission, the contest did provide "a boost for Valdres," in that it gave both the district and its dialect positive national exposure. Locally, as well, over the last decade and a half, an increasingly positive view of dialect use has left its mark, and many Valdres residents, young and old, now use dialect in everyday writing, as well as in speech. Primary sites for written dialect use are text messaging and social media, where many people tell me that using anything other than dialect would be ridiculous (more on this in Strand 2019).

Another growing site for written dialect use is in tourism development and marketing, which have capitalized on the district's and dialect's positive national reputation. Shortly after the contest win, Valdresmål began popping up in marketing of all kinds, from the local summer rock festival to a now-defunct local dating website to high-end artisanal foods and crafts. Recruiters for the hospitality sector also told me that they preferred to hire dialect speakers, as they believed it helped promote a local image of tradition and authenticity. These overtly economic uses of the dialect are all part of a growing global trend toward the commodification of local linguistic resources (Duchêne and Heller 2012), particularly in tourist markets, including places like Quebec (Heller 2003), Barcelona (Pujolar 2006), Pittsburgh (Johnstone 2009), and Michigan's Upper Peninsula (Remlinger 2017), among others. Chapter 5 will discuss dialect commodification in Valdres in much greater detail.

Stepping back to see the dialect contest in broad context, there is a fairly wide range of social, historical, ideological, and economic factors that, in combination, have opened up a space for the dialect renaissance now easily observable in Valdres. Among them is the more than 150-year saga of language planning in Norway, involving two written norms with competing nationalist claims, the popular rejection of a spoken standard, and promotion of dialect diversity as a part of Norway's *kulturarv* (cultural heritage) in recent decades, which helps to account for the strong, emotional feelings people attach to non-normative regional language in Norway. The use and acceptance of non-normative dialects in national broadcast media has also increased dramatically in this century, and the historical ubiquity of metalinguistic discourse in Norway has also produced a small but popular industry of language-focused reporting and entertainment in mass media. All of these things are part of the dominant cultural, political, and language-ideological environment that fostered the *Reiseradioen* dialect contest.

The 2005 contest also produced very particular local meanings in Valdres. Valdresmål speakers of all ages were excited to be in the running throughout the contest, and they were beyond proud when their dialect was voted Norway's most popular. Mass-mediated, national discourses and practices valuing and promoting dialect diversity have contributed to twenty-first-century dialect revalorization in Valdres, facilitated in part by substantial emotional investments in "traditional," rural language and culture. Yet despite a consistent social aesthetic of language across generational lines, winning the dialect popularity contest also brought to the fore generational differences in language ideologies, pitting some amount of dialect purism against youths' innovative, playful, and sometimes simply ordinary language mixing.

The generational contrasts in attitudes toward legitimate or acceptable dialect use in Valdres may ultimately point to underlying differences in how people conceptualize what a dialect is. What makes a regional dialect a dialect? Where and how do we draw the line between normative and non-normative language? These are thorny questions for linguists and laypeople alike. In Valdres, many older residents emphasize how certain Valdresmål features are falling out of use in favor of more normative ones, which leads them to evaluate contemporary Vallers as a deficient dialect that is no longer properly "local" or "traditional." In so doing, they operationalize a popular, long-standing definition of "dialect" as a regional way of speaking with a specific combination of distinctive, non-normative linguistic forms, from words and grammar to pronunciation. Many younger speakers, however, appear to have a much different understanding of "dialect" – one that counts the remaining non-normative features of local speech, of which there are many, as sufficiently different from normative, urban varieties to still be considered a distinct dialect even when they are, at times, used in combination with normative forms. Within this conceptualization of "dialect," using markedly local words and grammar is still critical, but it is not all or nothing; not every possible word or grammatical form has to be distinctly local in every utterance in order to be counted as legitimate dialect.

Either way, social pressure and economic incentives to use Valdres dialect have only strengthened in the aftermath of the dialect popularity contest, and it has become a central, perhaps even defining, component of local identity and branding. As Valdresmål speakers and residents have put their traditional dialect to new uses in recent decades, they have effectively reinvented it, drawing from the past to leverage local language as a resource that positions them as a small but unified community forging a viable future.

THE FOLLOWING CHAPTERS

The chapters that follow provide deeper context for and trace contemporary uses of Valdresmål. Chapter 2, titled "A Tradition of Language Politics," sketches the historical context for the unique sociolinguistic climate of contemporary Norway, including the development of its two distinct, official written norms and the more recent turn toward spoken dialect as a critical facet of social identity and style. This chapter discusses the politically fraught nature of (written) language standardization and planning, which figured centrally in Norwegian national politics from the mid-1800s to the mid-1900s, and which has been described as producing a natural sociolinguistic laboratory in Norway. Additionally, it uses participant observation and interviews from Valdres to address how the rules of (formal) writing can be variable, and how Norwegians learn and negotiate the dual written norms alongside spoken dialect today. Based on ethnographic data, it concludes that long-standing beliefs about the "natural" links between dialect and written Nynorsk are shifting, which has made dialect even more important and valuable in the social politics of language today than it has been in the past.

Turning more directly toward spoken dialect use, Chapter 3, "Dialect as Style, Stereotype, and Resistance," directly links the local and national contexts introduced in the first two chapters and expands on the use of dialect in national media, incorporating interview data and media examples related to local celebrities' use of Valdresmål on television and in other highly public venues. The analysis in this chapter shows how Norwegians in general and Valdres dialect speakers in particular are highly aware of the meaningfulness of dialectal differences in public interactional contexts, highlighting how dialect is positively interpreted as a part of "style" in contemporary Norway, as well as how Valdres speakers understand their use of the rural dialect with urban/non-dialect speakers to be a form of resistance to the perceived imposition of city people's language and culture.

Chapter 4, "Pro-dialect Ideology and the Dynamics of Language Change," takes a solidly linguistic turn, exploring what has changed in the Valdres dialect, what has been preserved, and why. To aid readers with what may be new linguistic terminology, a glossary to accompany this chapter is included as Appendix B. The chapter itself includes detailed analysis of early-twenty-first-century dialect change, based on recorded interview speech from more than forty native Valdres dialect speakers, born 1918–90. A combination of quantitative and qualitative linguistic analyses shows that the spoken language in Valdres is changing in multiple directions, both toward regional urban norms, as has been the case for at least a century, and also away from urban speech, as self-consciously non-normative, rural forms have come into favor among younger speakers. The linguistic analysis is contextualized through discussion of the kinds of language features and change many dialect speakers are aware of, which are contrasted with those that seem to be operating below the level of conscious awareness for most people. Carefully examining the interaction of normative and dialectal speech, as well as the two written norms for Norwegian, I conclude that contemporary dialect maintenance and change, including words, grammar, and pronunciation, are driven by both historic and more recently emergent language ideologies.

The final main chapter, Chapter 5, "A Must-Hear Attraction in the Nature and Culture Park," shifts focus away from more everyday, interactional spoken Valdresmål to new uses of dialect and changing contexts of use, particularly in relation to tourism growth. The use of written dialect in marketing local products and experiences grew substantially through the 2010s, as a new regional development organization and concept rebranded the traditional district of Valdres as "The Valdres Nature and Culture Park" (*Valdres Natur- og Kulturpark*, or VNK). Ethnographic examples show how traditional rural culture, landscape, and language are selectively but also rather arbitrarily incorporated into what is offered up in the contemporary visitor experience, as well as how the VNK has promoted the use of dialect in tourism and marketing in ways that are particularly well aligned with linguistic-anthropological analyses of "traditional" language being a source of both pride and profit in the global era. Ultimately, this chapter emphasizes how the commodification of Valdres dialect, culture, and landscape transforms those very same things for both insiders and outsiders alike.

Chapter 6, "Finding the Local Past in a Global Future," offers a brief coda, reflecting on how language and culture have changed profoundly in Valdres as a result of both globalizing forces and local and national demographic trends, which are themselves interrelated. Returning to the problem of linguistic anxieties over the future of Valdresmål, I observe the myriad ways in which the dialect is presently thriving in traditional and new contexts, and also changing in the face of sociogeographic mobility and the pressures of late capitalism. The chapter and book end with an ethnographically informed consideration of current and near-future developments in Valdres language and culture.

CHAPTER TWO

A Tradition of Language Politics

Strong opinions about language abound in Norway and in Valdres. While Norway might have an outward reputation for political neutrality, no one I have talked to claims to be entirely neutral when it comes to speaking and writing Norwegian. Just a few minutes into an interview with Eva, a life-long Valdres resident, she quipped that "these half-fancy people [from Valdres], when they talk in city language (*bymål*), I call it Home-Danish (*heimedansk*)." Eva was well into her seventies, but she was still born more than 100 years after Danish control of Norway ended in 1814 and decades after Norway gained full independence from Sweden in 1905. And yet, in 2008, she was deriding her neighbors' mixing of traditional Valdres dialect with words and grammar from outside the district as a misguided use of "Danish."

Along with language and dialect, I also spoke with Eva about growing up in Valdres, her passion for traditional folk art, and her family, even looking through some old photographs from a farm that once belonged to ancestors we had in common. At every opportunity, though, Eva delighted in expressing her pride in Valdres and Valdresmål, her fondness for Nynorsk (the minority written norm), and her humor-cloaked contempt for city talk and Bokmål (the more widely used written norm). In the second half of our interview, when my questions eventually turned directly toward reading and writing Norwegian, Eva let her sharp opinions fly. "Bokmål? It's a degenerate form of Danish," she told me matter-of-factly with a wry smile on her broad, wrinkled face, driving home her earlier assessment of "impure" spoken dialect. But why, after nearly 200 years of independence from Denmark, was this still so relevant? Bokmål and Nynorsk have both been officially endorsed as legitimate forms for written Norwegian since 1885, but, like Norway's diverse spoken dialects, its legally equal written norms are clearly not considered equivalent in practice.

Eva preferred to read and write in Nynorsk, which is often seen as more closely aligned with the spoken dialects of Central and Western Norway in terms of spelling and grammar. This belief was common among dialect speakers I talked to, especially middle-aged and older Valdres residents. But Eva took her preference for Valdresmål and Nynorsk to something of an activist level, both as a member of the local Nynorsk organization (Valdres Mållag) and in her day-to-day affairs:

(1) E: *E kjøpe før eksempel kun . heilmjølk*
For example, I only buy whole milk
(2) *før der står det MJØLK på kartongé.*
because it says *MJØLK* (MILK) on the carton.
(3) T: *Mm-mm.*
Mm-hm.
(4) E: *Det står HEIL.*
It says *HEIL* (WHOLE).
(5) T: *Ja.*
Yes.
(6) E: *Og så kjøpe e – visst e ska kjøpe me saft og sleke ting*
And I buy – if I'm going to buy juice or that kind of thing
(7) *kjøpe e ifrå Lærum før dei bruka Nynorsk.*
I buy from Lærum [brand] because they use Nynorsk.
(8) T: *Dei gjere det ja?*
Oh, they do?
(9) E: *Og det seie e då med høy røst før kor gong e betala*
And I say it loudly every time I [go to] pay
(10) *før eksempel ved kassa og slekt. "E må kjøpe slek*
like at the cash register and such. "I have to buy this kind
(11) *fordi at her e det på Nynorsk."*
because it's in Nynorsk."

As Eva implies in lines 1–4, there are different ways of saying and writing "whole milk" in Norwegian, and this is an illustrative example of how Bokmål and Nynorsk differ, as well as how Nynorsk sometimes corresponds well to spoken dialects, including Valdresmål. "Whole milk" is written as *heilmjølk* in Nynorsk and as *helmelk* in Bokmål. Nynorsk *heilmjølk* also happens to match the rural Valdres dialect pronunciation very closely (/hɑjlmjøɫk/), while Bokmål *helmelk* matches local pronunciations in urban Eastern Norway, including Oslo (/heːlmɛlk/). In Valdres, with its long tradition of dairy farming, talking about milk and the labor of milking makes this a high-frequency and culturally central word, and there is special attention paid to how it is pronounced or spelled. This is so much the case that Norway's largest dairy brand, Tine, has intentionally used the Nynorsk *heilmjølk* on cartons of whole milk sold in Valdres, among other places, to successfully market to consumers like Eva, who prefer to buy milk that reflects their dialect and other linguistic and cultural allegiances. And while Eva may have been more zealous than most in her preference for Nynorsk-labeled products – bringing this up at every cash register transaction, as she claims in lines 9–11 above – it is certainly the case that many people in Valdres and throughout the country engage in everyday talk and action that are, directly or indirectly, linked to a long and highly politicized history of language planning at the national level.

This chapter relates some of that history and explores how two centuries of Norwegian language planning remain relevant – sometimes acutely so – in local language attitudes and linguistic practice. It shows how, over the last 1,000 years, very particular historical circumstances contributed to national language projects and policies, and to dominant beliefs people have about written and spoken Norwegian. The Norwegian and Valdres cases also demonstrate that shifting political and economic circumstances produce shifting linguistic ideologies and preferences over time, including differences across generational lines, which is a pattern seen globally. In this case, as Norwegian national prosperity and identity have become more secure, younger Valdres residents are less interested in the historically national*ist* debate over written language and instead more invested in their local dialect as a distinctive and valuable identity marker worth fighting for.

FROM OLD NORSE TO DANISH TO NEW NORWEGIAN

The contemporary Norwegian linguistic situation has resulted, in large part, from Norway's particular social and political history, including the imposition of Danish rule and language from the late 1300s until 1814. This, in turn, was followed by more than 150 years of fierce political debates over which ways of writing and speaking were best and most Norwegian, including a series of national language planning projects in the first half of the twentieth century, in which committees of language experts worked to "reform" and guide Bokmål and Nynorsk toward one another to eventually become a single written norm for all Norwegians. As Eva's comments above show, Danish control of Norway, debates pitting Bokmål against Nynorsk, and intense language planning have left their mark in Norwegian culture, where language politics – governmental and interpersonal alike – have become something of a tradition.

In looking a bit more deeply into Norwegian history, we can see that earlier, medieval events also helped set the stage for the contemporary linguistic and ideological landscape, beginning with a fairly sudden break from the strong and relatively stable written tradition of Old Norse, triggered by shifting royal alliances and epidemic disease in Norway during the thirteenth and fourteenth centuries. This deep historical context is critical for understanding how more recent language debates unfolded as they did, and why they were so acrimonious that their scars are still visible and audible today.

Looking back a thousand years or so, Christianity spread through Norway beginning around 1000 CE, and from approximately 1100 to the mid-1300s a series of Norwegian kings ruled the country from three different capital cities. Following the linguistics adage that "a language is a dialect with an army and a navy," Norwegian medieval linguistic history provides a clear illustration of how political power swings affected language norms, especially in writing. During the 1100s, the city of Trondheim, home to the Nidaros Cathedral, Norway's most important and well-known church, was both the religious and administrative center of Norway. Most formal education took place in monasteries and convents, and many children were taught to read and write in both Latin and Old Norse by monks in the major religious centers, of which Nidaros was foremost. As a result, the language used in Trondheim, in the northernmost part of Norway's southern lobe, functioned as the de facto norm for written Norwegian during the twelfth century (Lundeby and Torvik 1956). Early in the thirteenth century, however, King Håkon V moved the royal court to Bergen on Norway's western coast, making that city the new administrative capital. While in Bergen, Håkon V had many prominent foreign literary works translated into Norwegian (Seip 1979), and, because his scribes were from Bergen, these translations, as well as royal letters and edicts of various sorts, reflected the language varieties used in Western Norway at that time. Norway's administrative capital was moved yet again in 1299, this time to Oslo in Southeastern Norway, where it has remained since. Old Norse had had a relatively long and resilient written tradition during the Viking era, but there was far less linguistic stability in Norway during the High Middle Ages.

The Plague struck Norway in 1349–50, killing nearly half of the population and causing serious economic and political crises. The Black Death also proved to be an important turning point in Norwegian linguistic history, as a "more impressionistic way of writing" emerged in its aftermath (Vikør 1993, 52). Literacy rates declined along with economic prosperity and political autonomy, and German Hanseatic traders wielded linguistic and economic influence, particularly along the western coast, where massive Norwegian population loss during the Plague allowed them to monopolize foreign trade. Over time, German traders spread inward toward the capital of Oslo and gained a presence in all of Norway's major cities and towns.

In Bergen, Hanseatic traders created their largest colony, and, along with material goods, German language and culture flowed into Norway from its ports. Everyday business and social contact between German and Norwegian residents in Bergen and other cities necessarily resulted in a fair amount of linguistic contact. However, as in so many capitalist and colonial contexts (Heller and McElhinney 2017), contact did not take place on an equal footing, so cultural and linguistic exchange were far from balanced, with German having more power and influence. Perhaps as many as several thousand German words and affixes gradually made their way into Norwegian during this time (Skard 1976), altering the vocabulary and grammar of spoken Norwegian in much of the country, but particularly in Western Norway.

In 1380, Norway entered a political union with Denmark that quickly turned into the rule of Norway *by* Denmark, which persisted for over 400 years. Initially, Danish administrators made some efforts to use the Norwegian language in Norway (Kolsrud 1979), but, from 1450 on, Danish dominated as the language of government and official correspondence. Around 1500, priests in Oslo and Trondheim began using and teaching written Danish (Lundeby and Torvik 1956), further pushing written Norwegian into disuse. Few rural Norwegians learned literacy skills during this time, and, in the population at large, those with the highest social status were either themselves Danes or had learned Danish as the language of reading, writing, and education, more broadly. This process of *language shift* (i.e., one language being displaced by another in some or all contexts) was helped along by the post-Reformation church, which, in addition to preaching and teaching in Danish, used bibles and other religious texts printed exclusively in Denmark, where printing presses first arrived in 1481, long before the 1643 arrival of the first press in Norway. Throughout Europe and beyond, early printed texts contributed greatly to the creation, normalization, and standardization of "languages-of-power" within nation-states (Anderson 1991). By the end of the Middle Ages in Norway, written Norwegian had virtually disappeared from use, and Danish had taken its place – a fact that is at once an accident of history (epidemics and royal alliances are hardly predictable) and the source of considerable linguistic and social resentments that have persisted into modern times.

At the beginning of the nineteenth century, most of the Norwegian population was still working on family farms, and Norway remained under Danish rule. However, Norwegian timber and fishing exports were growing rapidly, leading to political and economic tensions within the small but growing Norwegian bourgeoisie. Regional alliances in Northern Europe were shaken up in the first decade of the 1800s by the Napoleonic Wars, which cut off thriving trade relations between Norway and Britain and caused an economic crisis. Norwegian nobles and tradespeople organized to demand independence from Denmark, and, after tense negotiations among Denmark, Sweden, and an ad hoc Norwegian parliament, the Dano-Norwegian union ended in 1814, with control of Norway's external affairs ceded to Sweden and the new Norwegian government in charge of domestic matters.

In Norway's cities, many prominent writers and politicians were oriented to romantic nationalist movements then popular elsewhere in Europe, and, in these circles, Danish – the official language of Norway for several centuries by that point – came to be seen as an imposition on Norway's national identity and character. The 1814 Constitution thus called for the exclusive use of "the Norwegian language" in the newly formed government, but this presented a serious practical problem: Old Norse had long ago fallen out of use in writing, and while distinctly Norwegian dialects were still spoken throughout the country, especially by peasants in outlying areas, the educated upper classes spoke largely Danish in terms of words and grammar, but with Norwegian pronunciations. Scholars and politicians proposed a variety of plans for the Norwegianization of written Danish for use in official business and literary works in the first decades after the break with Denmark. But a turning point came in 1836, when the young linguist Ivar Aasen published an essay advocating for an entirely "new" Norwegian written language to be developed from the "old" dialects spoken by rural peasants, effectively rejecting the Dano-Norwegian language used by wealthy urbanites as inappropriate for the role of the national language of Norway.

To launch this revolutionary project, Aasen traveled around the country in the 1840s, documenting a great many of Norway's rural dialects and consciously avoiding cities (Jahr 2014). He worked to analyze these dialects, particularly their linguistic relationships to written Old Norse, publishing an initial grammar in 1848 and a dictionary in 1850. Aasen then went to work on synthesizing Norway's many dialects and weeding out obvious borrowings from German and Danish to produce a new, unified written standard in his 1864 *Norsk Grammatik* (*Norwegian Grammar*). Aasen called his version of Norwegian *Landsmaal* (language of the land/country), which, like its English gloss, carries a dual meaning: both the language of the nation-state and the language of rural areas. Aasen's Landsmaal, which eventually came to be called Nynorsk (literally "new Norwegian"), was quickly put to use by fellow Norwegian nationalists, including some prominent literary writers, inciting intense linguistic, social, and political debates that continued for the next hundred years.

SOCIAL CONFLICT AND LANGUAGE PLANNING

By 1905, when Norway finally regained full political sovereignty, language reform efforts were well under way. Laws supporting the use of local spoken dialects for instruction in the classroom were in place as early as 1878 (Jahr 1984), and Parliament endorsed the use of Aasen's written Landsmaal in government and schools in 1885. In 1892, local school boards were granted the authority to choose either Landsmaal or Dano-Norwegian as the written standard for schoolbooks and student writing in their own districts, with new teachers required to pass a Landsmaal exam as part of their training starting in 1902 (Jahr 2014). In Valdres, all of the six local school boards had adopted Landsmaal as their primary written standard by 1919, among the earliest in Eastern Norway to do so, which Eva proudly related during our interview in 2008.

On the other side of the debate, shortly after the end of the union with Sweden, language reformers took on the project of more fully Norwegianizing and standardizing the Dano-Norwegian written norm, based on the speech of well-educated urban elites. In 1907, new orthographic (spelling) and grammatical standards were legally approved, and the Dano-Norwegian written language was given a new name: *Riksmaal* (language of the land/territory). Ultimately, then, schoolchildren throughout Norway were acquiring literacy in two newly developed and newly authorized writing systems, both of which were quite different from the ways their parents and essentially all earlier Norwegian authors had written.

Following the officialization of Riksmaal reforms, the Norwegian government also made it obligatory for all secondary school students to pass an exam in Landsmaal as part of national graduation requirements. This move provoked considerable resentment among urban Riksmaal adherents, who referred to Landsmaal derogatorily as *fjøsmaal* (barn language) – a position quite the opposite of the admiration for rural language we see a century later, as discussed in Chapter 1 on the 2005 dialect popularity contest. The year 1907 also marked the founding of *Riksmaalsforbundet* (The Riksmaal Association), which was largely a response to the coalescence of Landsmaal activists around the country into their own national organization, *Noregs Maallag* (Norway's Language Association), the year prior. The conflict over Norway's national language was by this time bitterly entrenched, and, crucially, it had just as much to do with history, culture, and social relations as it did with language itself.

In the early twentieth century, support for Aasen's Landsmaal continued to grow, especially in Western and Central Norway, but so did the anti-Landsmaal/pro-Riksmaal movement, with neither side on a clear path toward winning the prize of becoming the sole official national language. Out of this situation, some relatively moderate voices began advocating for Landsmaal and Riksmaal to be unified into a "common Norwegian," or *Samnorsk*. Among the earliest and most influential Samnorsk supporters was professor and folklorist Moltke Moe (1909), who, in an essay titled "Nationality and Culture," argued for a linguistically and socially unified path forward:

> Neither [language] can wipe out the other or throw it out of the country. We cannot dispense with either our old history or our recent history, cannot exclude either city or country. Both must participate, each from its own side, in reaching the great goal: a common Norwegian language, grown out of the living dialects of the cities as well as the countryside.

As a possible solution to the seemingly intractable Landsmaal-Riksmaal, urban-rural tensions, the idea of Samnorsk was politically appealing to many in government, and, beginning in 1909, a series of language planning committees were appointed, charged with bringing together the two Norwegian written norms for the sake of the nation.

The actual work of synthesizing Riksmål and Landsmål (as they were known after spelling reforms in 1917 allowed *å* to replace *aa* for the /ɔ/ vowel) required sociolinguistic analysis of both existing written norms and spoken dialects throughout the country. This was no small or easy task, and language reforms happened in dribs and drabs through the early decades. Rather than always selecting just one "correct" way of writing, which tends to be the more common strategy in language planning and standardization projects, Norwegian planners from early on decided to allow writers flexibility when there was strong support in spoken dialects for more than one spelling or grammatical pattern. For instance, from 1917, Riksmål had two officially endorsed spellings for "clean," either *ren* or *rein*, which reflected differences in pronunciation that fell out mostly along the social lines of elite versus working class (both rural and urban), respectively, and this pattern held systematically for other similar words, including "whole" (*hel* or *heil*), which we saw in Eva's milk carton example above. The *ei* spelling, reflecting a diphthongal (two-vowel-sound) pronunciation, was already used in Landsmål, so allowing it to also be optionally used in Riksmål effectively brought the two written norms a bit closer together.

Grammatically, a similar move allowed for the optional use of feminine gender in Riksmål, rather than requiring the use of the so-called "common" grammatical gender, so that Riksmål users could write *ei bok* and *boka* ("a-fem. book" and "the-fem. book") or *en bok* and *boken* ("a-com. book" and "the-com. book"), the former found in most working-class speech and the latter primarily in elite, urban speech, as well as in Danish. In step with most rural Norwegian dialects, Landsmål already required use of feminine articles and other markers for grammatically feminine nouns, but it had previously required different rules for "strong" and "weak" feminine forms, a distinction that was gradually falling out of use in spoken language. Here, language planners were able to bring Landsmål closer to Riksmål with the optional simplification of feminine noun declension into a single pattern. These are just two small examples of many hundreds of changes, and if the process of language planning, standardization, and unification sounds complicated here, be assured that it was!

Adding to the complexity were the social politics surrounding language planning work in Norway. As political scientist Gregg Bucken-Knapp has argued, the promotion of and preference for Norwegian written norms in the twentieth century was very closely tied to national political parties' goals and values (Bucken-Knapp 2003). Perhaps the clearest example of the incorporation of language into a party platform was that of the Labor Party (*Arbeiderpartiet*) in the 1930s, where "the class struggle was reinterpreted to include not only the economic but also the linguistic liberation of the common people" (Haugen 1966, 104). As the largest national party in the 1930s, the Labor Party advocated for what it called "the people's language" – the speech of rural peasants and urban proletarians – to continue to be incorporated into both written norms, and for the two norms to eventually be brought together into a single national standard. Both linguistic and social reforms were promoted through the rhyming slogan *By og land, hand i hand!* (Town and country, hand in hand), which, as Jahr notes, uses the common working-class form *hand*, with a low, unrounded vowel, rather than the more elite (and Riksmål/Danish) form *hånd*, with a mid-back, rounded vowel (Jahr 2014, 112). In 1938, the Labor Party was successful in shepherding through what were widely agreed to be radical spelling reforms that brought many urban, working-class speech forms into the written languages and further marginalized elite, "literary" Dano-Norwegian spellings and grammar as either optional or directly nonstandard, leading to fresh outrage among Riksmål supporters. It was also during this period that Riksmål was renamed *Bokmål* (book language) and Landsmål as *Nynorsk* (new Norwegian), names that remain in use today.

In 1941, political life in Norway was abruptly cut off by the invasion of German forces during World War II. Following the common crisis and tragedy of the war, Norwegian political values and agendas, including those related to language, were significantly altered, and cooperation seemed possible in linguistic matters, as elsewhere. Despite passionate pre-war support for Landsmål/Nynorsk and intense debates between Landsmål/Nynorsk and Riksmål/Bokmål supporters through the 1930s, a 1946 poll showed that 80 percent of Norwegians wanted a single written norm (Haugen 1966, 165). To this end, a new national Language Commission (*Språknemnd*) was assembled, and its members worked to devise additional changes to both written norms with the goal of finally merging them completely.

Amidst major rebuilding and rapid urbanization in the 1950s, however, more city-dwelling Norwegians, particularly in Oslo, began organizing more effectively in support of retaining Riksmål/Bokmål and against the Samnorsk (common Norwegian) project, complaining that "[language] planning is resulting in a language which no one speaks" (Haugen 1966, 292). Of course, written language and spoken language are never perfectly aligned, but pro-Bokmål activists were angered that reforms to written Norwegian continued to diverge from the forms of both writing and speech that had been dominant in urban Eastern Norway for many centuries. And their well-funded campaign against the Samnorsk planning project was ultimately effective, resulting first in an official pause in language planning work and then its eventual abandonment in the mid-1960s.

Since then, the two written norms, Nynorsk and Bokmål, have coexisted as legal equals, and debates around written language have figured somewhat less centrally in political life. Turning away from the Samnorsk fight, the 1970s and 1980s brought a new pro-dialect movement led by Noregs Mållag (the national Nynorsk association) and, especially, its youth organization, Noregs Målungdom, promoted with the slogan "Speak dialect, write Nynorsk."

That is exactly what many people I talked to in Valdres were doing in the first decade of the twenty-first century, including Eva. However, the local language landscape in Valdres is far from uniform. While Nynorsk remains the primary language of early literacy instruction in most Valdres schools, Bokmål is preferred by many adults and high school students, which has to do in large part with the longer history of written Dano-Norwegian and its unbroken dominance in popular print media. In M.M. Bakhtin's terms, this is a situation of official and profound *heteroglossia* (Bakhtin 1984), with many different varieties of Norwegian coexisting, interacting, and, at times, in competition with one another. Bakhtin was most concerned with language variation in literary works (Dostoevsky's novels, especially), but he keenly observed the multitude of social, political, and regional perspectives and contexts that inhere in different varieties of a language and that cannot be entirely thrown off by successive groups of speakers.

The history of language planning and politics sketched so far in this chapter is thus still part of what it means to use any particular form of Norwegian today. But also, having the freedom to choose a preferred way of writing or speaking, without significant social or economic risk, has become part of a distinctly Norwegian cultural tradition, one that linguists have described as both a sociolinguistic paradise and a natural, ever-evolving sociolinguistic laboratory. Nevertheless, Norwegians' linguistic choices today are anything but a free-for-all, and people in Valdres still have to navigate complex cultural tensions surrounding dialect, Nynorsk, and Bokmål, even if they are usually subtler and less contentious than in the past.

LIVING AND LEARNING IN THE SOCIOLINGUISTIC LABORATORY

Because there is no single, uniform, standard written Norwegian, a choice has to be made every time a Norwegian writer puts pen to paper or fingers to keyboard. Will they write in Bokmål, the more common written form, sometimes associated with urban people and life? Will they write in Nynorsk, which is perceived to be closer to everyday speech in rural, Central, and Western Norway, but which also has a reputation for being difficult and stilted? Or will they mix words and grammar that might be found in Bokmål, Nynorsk, or both with nonstandard spellings to write approximately as they speak? The answer depends on the context, of course, and once-difficult choices may become unselfconscious habits over time. Today, a mix of standard and nonstandard, often dialectal forms prevails in the informal digital writing that is central to everyday life in a smartphone-centric world. But in formal writing, either Bokmål or Nynorsk is called for, and, while both come with historical baggage, these days the baggage seems much heavier for Nynorsk. "It's like it's neutral when it's Bokmål," a long-time local journalist explained to me, "but when you write Nynorsk it's very political."

Eva, the fervent Nynorsk supporter who called Bokmål a degenerate form of Danish at the beginning of this chapter, clearly embraced the political nature of the minority written norm, forcefully advocating for Nynorsk at every opportunity. She was not alone in this enduring fight, as evidenced by strong membership numbers and a variety active projects in Valdres's language associations. But many of the Nynorsk users I talked to were more interested in the aesthetics of Nynorsk than in its politics, and plenty of devoted Valdres dialect speakers also told me they preferred writing and reading Bokmål. If the social experiment of language planning has not quite led to a sociolinguistic utopia (Mæhlum and Røyneland 2009), it has nevertheless produced opportunities for linguistic choice, variation, resistance, and reflection that are unique and distinctly Norwegian.

Valdres was among the many rural places Ivar Aasen visited during his national dialect surveys in the mid-1800s, logging three visits and documenting thousands of words and expressions (published as Aasen 2002), which he used, along with many others, as he worked to develop the new Norwegian written norm expressly designed to be closer to Norway's spoken dialects. This original understanding of Nynorsk and its "natural" relationship to Valdresmål remains strong, and, in one way or another, it has pervaded nearly every conversation I have had about Nynorsk in Valdres, with older and younger people alike, and with both Bokmål users and Nynorsk users. Among the latter, the dialect-Nynorsk link was a perfectly obvious explanation for their preferences. Over cups of steaming peppermint tea (not coffee, for once!), Audunn, a thirty-ish local theater producer, laid out the linguistic logic for me:

> *E bruka nynorsk. Det ha e gjort heile tie. Og det e det som ha vørte naturle, det e det – det ha vørte mi skriftlige dialekt, rett og slett. Det e kji naturle før me å skrive bokmål. Så klart kan e skrive på bokmål, e har kji noko grammatiske problem med det, men. Men skrivestemma mi e på nynorsk. Det kjenne e, kjenne e veldi på, at det e det so fell naturle før me. Og ganske dialektnær nynorsk i dei – så langt det går an innafor dei grammatikalske rammudn.*
>
> I use Nynorsk. I always have. And it's what's become natural, it's what – it's simply become my written dialect. It's not natural for me to write Bokmål. Of course I can write in Bokmål, I don't have any grammatical problem with it, but. But my writing voice is in Nynorsk. I feel that, I feel it very strongly, that it comes naturally for me. And pretty dialect-near Nynorsk to the – as much as possible within the grammatical limits.

Here, Audunn also alludes to the flexibility of Nynorsk and its many internal options for certain words and morphological patterns (plural or past-tense suffixes, for example). During ethnographic fieldwork, I attended a weekly, evening Nynorsk class for adults, where my classmates and I learned that, given its many optional forms, one of the most important demands in writing Nynorsk "correctly" is to be consistent, choosing forms that "match" one another throughout a piece of writing. Like many in Valdres, Audunn managed this by consistently choosing the words and spellings in Nynorsk that were closest to Valdresmål whenever such options were available.

But, like any other standardized language, the official Nynorsk wordlist does not include every word and pronunciation found in Valdresmål or any particular dialect. Recall that Aasen deliberately weeded out linguistic forms that he judged to be (too) Danish or German, even though they might have been in regular use in rural Norway at the time, and many remain so today. While Eva and Audunn were content to use Nynorsk words that were not also part of their own habitual spoken repertoire, others struggled – both practically and ideologically – with reading and writing some of Nynorsk's less familiar words and grammar. As I chatted with John, a local entrepreneur, in his shop along the main street in Valdres's commercial and administrative center, he told me he was a committed dialect speaker, having grown up in a more rural part of the valley, and he was eager to see Valdresmål reinvigorated through more public use, including in commercial marketing. But he was less keen on Nynorsk and skeptical of its supposedly obvious connection to rural dialects like his own:

> *E synst ikkji nynorsken fanga gøtt nok valdresdialekte uansett. Den e eit opp – for me eit oppkonstruert språk uansett. Altså det e kji slek e prata. Fordi om det e sikkert den er nærmere så føle e at det bli omtrent akkuratt det sama. E ser ikkji heilt den klare sammenhengen der som mange andre ser. Det er ein del sånne ord som e heilt unaturle for me å bruke i nynorsk. Som e syns liksom då e det meir naturle å bruke bokmålsord fordi at dei høyre du i så mange andre sammenhenga lell.*
>
> I don't think Nynorsk captures the Valdres dialect well enough anyway. It's a ma – for me a made-up language no matter what. Like it's not how I talk. Because even though it surely is closer I still feel that it's just about exactly the same. I don't really see the clear connection there that many others see. There are a bunch of words that are completely unnatural for me to use in Nynorsk. That I think like then it's more natural to use Bokmål words because you hear those in so many other contexts anyway.

John therefore chose to write in Bokmål most of the time when standard writing was called for, but in more casual contexts, he often wrote in a way that reflected his spoken language, using non-normative (i.e., non-Bokmål and non-Nynorsk) spellings and words to capture the sounds and sentiments of Valdresmål.

Many, if not most, younger people in Valdres shared this writing-choice pattern, as well as John's ambivalence toward Nynorsk. Teachers in central Valdres told me their students, especially in the upper grades, increasingly preferred Bokmål for schoolwork, and, despite having had Nynorsk as the default written language in Valdres's rural elementary schools, most selected Bokmål as their primary language when given the choice upon entering the district's sole secondary school (*Valdres Vidaregåendeskule*) – even those who were proud dialect speakers. This situation mystified many in the pro-Nynorsk camp, including some teachers, who insisted that it made much more sense for Valdresmål-speaking students to write and read in Nynorsk. But others allowed themselves a bit more freedom to observe and reflect on young people's language practices with less judgment or worry. Among them was Mette, a secondary school teacher who grew up in rural Valdres, attended university and worked in the Oslo area for some time, and then returned to Valdres to start a family. After teaching in Valdres's secondary school for quite a few years, Mette's view of her students' linguistic choices, which were different from her own, gradually shifted:

> *Altså det har e heile tie vøre heilt helli overbevist um at <u>det</u> er eit stert forhold. E ha vøre heilt sikker på at […] før uss som bur i Valdres så e nynorsk […] den mest nærliggande målførmen. O ein målførm som kan <u>hjølpe uss</u> å bevare dialekta våres. Det har e heile tie trudd. Men så når e ser på desse here elevadn mine at no e e litt usikker. E e litt sånn – før som sagt det e veldi få tå dei som bruka nynorsk. Men samtidi så muntli så – så syns e at dei e ganske – e syns dei prata vallers mange tå dei. O e flinke te å halde på det. Så e berre lure på om den forbindelsen kanskje ikkji e så sterk som e har trudd. Eller om, om det berre er ein fase dei – altså at det at dei har hatt nynorsk på skula veldi mange tå dei då, frå fyste te tiende klasse. At det ha vøre med på å hjølpe dei te at dei har den dialektbruken som dei har no når dei e komne hit. Kanskje?*
>
> So I've always been totally, completely convinced that <u>that</u> is a strong relationship. I've been completely sure that […] for us who live in Valdres that Nynorsk is […] the closest language. And a

> language that can <u>help us</u> preserve our dialect. I've always believed that. But so now when I look at my students here, that I'm a little uncertain. I'm a little – because as I said there are very few of them who use Nynorsk. But at the same time in speech now I think that they're pretty – I think they speak Vallers many of them. And are good at keeping it up. So I just wonder about whether the connection maybe isn't as strong as I've thought. Or whether it's just a phase they – like that it's that they've had Nynorsk in school many of them, from first to tenth grade. That that's helped them to have [as much] dialect use as they do when they've gotten here. Maybe?

As she told me this, Mette's voice seemed strained at times, and it was clear that the ideological conflict was real for her. Sitting behind the expansive teacher's desk at the front of her classroom, as someone with specialized training in language and literature and charged with teaching those subjects to her students, Mette struggled to reconcile dominant and enduring Norwegian beliefs about Nynorsk, Bokmål, and dialect with her own first-hand observations. Linguistic ideology failed to match up neatly with sociolinguistic reality. And it was difficult for Mette, a well-educated, pro-Nynorsk, pro-dialect writer-speaker, to suggest that the Nynorsk-dialect relationship was less natural or necessary than she had been socialized to be "totally, completely convinced" of. The complex legacy of Norwegian language planning and politics influenced both Mette's direct experiences with contemporary language use in Valdres and her feelings around those experiences.

Within the ranks of Mette's current and recent students, though, most were less troubled by their generation's apparent drift away from Nynorsk. Stian, the high school student and musical theater performer introduced in the previous chapter, was vocal about his preference and affection for Valdresmål, but he saw Nynorsk as something quite different and less important. "I think dialect is much nicer than Nynorsk," he told me. "So if people here were to start speaking Nynorsk it wouldn't be the same. And, as I said, it's about people's identity." For Stian, Nynorsk was simply not something he felt attached to in the same way as dialect. Even though he had learned to read and write in Nynorsk in elementary school, he did not see it as a meaningful part of his identity.

And I heard similar sentiments from other young dialect speakers in their teens and twenties, including Øystein, a young entrepreneur and folk artist. When we sat down for an interview at a local café one afternoon, Øystein was in the process of permanently moving back to Valdres after living in Oslo for several years, and he had just launched a slick new website for his fledgling company, which I noticed was written in Bokmål with an additional English-language option but no Nynorsk. As I had heard him do often before, Øystein spoke in Valdres dialect during our long and meandering interview, and he shared with me that he felt he had spoken less dialect as a teenager but, in his early twenties, self-consciously began to use more of the old Valdresmål words and grammar he heard growing up. When it came to written language, though, he shared Stian's nonchalance.

> *Du kan seie at for me, så e det mykji mindre viktig å halde fast på nynorsken enn det e på Valdresdialekt. Nynorsken e ein mykji mindre del tå identiteten min enn dialekte. […] O det e mykji meir normert, det med skriftspråk i Norge. Det e mykji meir uttrykk for styrke um du prata dialekt enn um du skriv Nynorsk, syns e då.*
>
> You could say that for me, it's much less important to stick with Nynorsk than with Valdres dialect. Nynorsk is a much smaller part of my identity than dialect. […] And it's much more standardized, written language in Norway. It's much more an expression of strength if you speak dialect than if you write Nynorsk, I think anyway.

Identity and strength were also, of course, of central concern in the early years of Norwegian independence, when Nynorsk was developed and most fervently advocated for. However, in the twenty-first century, in a period of general political stability and economic good fortune for Norway, national identity can often be taken for granted. Yet people in Valdres and many other "small" and rural communities in Norway and around the world share the sense that the future of distinctive local cultures and identities is less certain, and efforts to preserve and revalue local language are one response. This is perhaps a less overtly political project, but, in the Norwegian context, it can also be understood as an extension of the deeply entrenched history of linguistic differentiation and contestation, this time with local rather than national pride at stake.

THE TRADITION LIVES ON

As the social, political, and economic landscapes in Valdres and in Norway evolve, language continues to be a focal site for cultural investment and struggle. In some ways, it could hardly be otherwise, when so many generations have been socialized into a tradition of overt language politics as part and parcel of their native language acquisition process. "The life of a word is contained in its transfer from one mouth to another," Bakhtin wrote, "from one context to another context, from one social collective to another, from one generation to another generation. In this process, the word does not forget its own path and cannot completely free itself from the power of these concrete contexts into which it has entered" (1984, 202). So it is, in the inescapable heteroglossia of Norwegian sociolinguistic life, that learning any words at all entails learning their alternatives, both spoken and written, as well as the history and cultural meaningfulness of each of them.

Throughout the active language planning years of the nineteenth and twentieth centuries, it was clear that new political and economic contexts brought change, and that continues to be the case in the global era. Though it lingered in the background in the 2000s and 2010s, the old Nynorsk versus Bokmål fight seemed less top-of-mind for youth and younger adults, most of whom were much more interested in choices and changes in spoken Norwegian than they were in its written norms. Even the most pro-Nynorsk among them were decidedly moderate compared to people like Eva, who, in her seventies, still actively begrudged the Danish imposition that inheres in Bokmål and "city language." Younger dialect speakers like Audunn, who fervently claimed Nynorsk as her "writing voice," also conceded that, for certain purposes, Bokmål was a reasonable choice. "Nynorsk is a beautiful and lyrical language," Audunn told me, but she also found it "a little more awkward (*tungvint*)" in some contexts. "I think it's almost vandalism to use Nynorsk to explain chemical formulas with," she explained with a good laugh, as she related her choice of

Bokmål textbooks for science classes in her secondary and postsecondary education years.

The idea that Nynorsk is, or can be, awkward or difficult has persisted since its earliest development, and even among those who told me that they preferred *writing* Nynorsk, some also said that they would actually rather *read* Bokmål. John alluded to this above in his claim that Bokmål was preferable, because "you hear those [words] in so many other contexts anyway." And I heard similar sentiments from other Valdresmål speakers, including Sigrunn, a talented young athlete and pre-professional student, who said she always wrote in Nynorsk, but:

> *E e jo vørte ganske vant te å lesa bokmål for det e det n les stortsett då. Så det e nok kanskje – når e les nynorsk så e det nok kanskje fleire ord der e lure litt på. Når du kjem burt i nokon – <u>nokon</u> ord som e veldi forskjellige på nynorsk og bokmål, så e det kanskje nokon tå dei orde som e ikkji bruka vanlivis og som e ikkji heilt @@@ visste um. Så eh:: ja, slek sett, så e det jo nesten eh fleire ord på nynorsk som e ikkji kjenne enn i bokmål.*
>
> I've gotten pretty used to reading Bokmål because that's what you read for the most part. <u>So</u> it may be – when I read Nynorsk there are like maybe more words there [that] I wonder a little about. When you come across some – some words that are really different in Nynorsk and Bokmål, then it's maybe some of those words that I don't usually use and that I didn't really @@@ know about. So yeah, in that way there's almost uh more words in Nynorsk that I don't know than in Bokmål.

Thus, even while she favors Nynorsk on language-ideological grounds and in her own writing practice, she also feels some ambivalence toward Nynorsk's relatively more obscure lexicon, which is a consequence of its minority status and less frequent use in popular media. Eva, the long-time Nynorsk activist, pushed back against this, telling me in a well-rehearsed one-liner that "if everyone had read as much Nynorsk as Bokmål, then they wouldn't have any aversion to Nynorsk." This is probably true. However, I believe that the reasons for some younger Valdresmål speakers' disinterest in or dispreference for Nynorsk are multiple and more complex, and, though they are deeply tied to the specificities of the Norwegian context, they are not entirely unique.

Eva is right that Danish, Riksmål, and Bokmål's uninterrupted dominance in popular print media, like newspapers, novels, and – increasingly – online venues, as well as in marketing and business life, has been a critical factor in its own reproduction and many people's sense of it being more familiar and easier to use than Nynorsk. This is true in many other instances of language inequality, planning, and revitalization efforts, as well, elsewhere in Europe and beyond. While the Norwegian case is rather different from many for its intralinguistic variation and inequality, it is easy to observe that politically and economically dominant languages or language varieties with long literary traditions are very hard to compete with when it comes to popular adoption and visibility. For example, the case of Irish revitalization and its continued marginalization vis-à-vis English in popular culture and marketing in Ireland – despite widespread interest in its preservation – looks similar in many ways, as do a great many instances of indigenous language revitalization projects, where long-threatened, sometimes acutely endangered languages struggle against the inertia and political-economic power of colonial languages.

But it is not simply a numbers game, whether of market share or language-preference demographics. As Valdres residents, and especially younger dialect speakers, repeatedly alluded to, there is also the issue of Nynorsk's constructedness. It is, in fact, a written norm that was synthesized from the parts of many different spoken vernaculars. Regardless of its longevity, many people still perceive Nynorsk as unnatural and stilted in comparison to both everyday speech and written Bokmål, the latter of which has evolved from its Danish origins with somewhat less radical intervention. This, too, has been a confounding factor in other cases of language planning, even in places where language preservation or revitalization is popularly supported. In Corsica, for instance, a newly standardized written norm was widely called for but also widely criticized when it failed (perhaps predictably) to match up neatly with regional speech patterns anywhere on the island (Jaffe 1999). And, again, a multitude of similar cases can be found outside of Europe, as in the example of indigenous Kichwa language planning and revitalization in Ecuador, where speakers of lowland Kichwa dialects often reject the standardized Unified Kichwa norm, which they deem unnatural and "foreign" due to the prevalence of highland Kichwa forms it contains (Wroblewski 2021).

Finally, language politics in Norway have necessarily evolved beyond the Bokmål-Nynorsk fight that was central to defining the nation and Norwegianness in the nineteenth and twentieth centuries. With Norway's national political sovereignty and economic stability no longer in question, contemporary concerns around culture and identity in Norway increasingly focus on local traditions and distinctiveness. Nynorsk, drawing as it does from dozens of dialects from throughout Norway, is not perceived as local or distinctive in the way that Valdresmål is, and this is another reason why Nynorsk does not figure as centrally in language politics in Valdres today as it may have in the past. Here, global shifts have also made being and selling whatever is considered "local" a socially and economically profitable venture, and language is often a part of this trend in Norway as elsewhere. Indeed, as attention has largely turned toward spoken language and dialect revalorization within Valdres, local dialect use and change will be the focus of the remaining chapters of this book.

In closing this chapter, I would be remiss not to mention that tensions around Nynorsk and Bokmål do still flare up on occasion, even among young people, with the largest blaze in many decades ignited in the leadup to national elections in the fall of 2021. Intending to provoke, the youth arm of the conservative Progress Party (*Fremskrittspartiet*) launched a viral campaign with the slogan "F**k Nynorsk." (Linguistically, *føkk* is a Norwegianized borrowing of English "fuck," so it works equally well in both languages.) As readers will by now fully expect, such an overtly political and vulgar attack on Nynorsk ignited a fresh, red-hot debate over the value of the minority written norm and its rightful place in Norwegian culture and institutions, particularly, in this case, in schools. In the aftermath, in both national and local media coverage, it has been clear that many speaking out in support of Nynorsk through this recent episode were not Nynorsk users themselves but instead dialect speakers who forcefully articulated the position that, for them, much of Nynorsk's value is tied to the ways it supports local and regional dialect use and preservation. The 2021 incident also had the effect of driving up membership in *Noregs Mållag*, the national Nynorsk organization, to record-high numbers (Noregs Mållag 2021). So, while spoken dialect may increasingly be the focus for language activists in this century, the embers continue to glow under the Nynorsk-Bokmål fire.

CHAPTER THREE

Dialect as Style, Stereotype, and Resistance

Speaking dialect is not just people's "normal" or "natural" way of talking. It may feel that way sometimes, but in most Norwegian contexts dialect also signals a whole mess of things – most obviously, where someone likely grew up, but also so much more, because places are ideologically linked to certain kinds of people, activities, values, and various moments and meanings from their history. As mentioned in Chapter 1, these kinds of associations for Valdresmål include things like farming, folk music, and qualities of friendliness, trustworthiness, and steadiness. This complex bundle of language, practice, and personality traits is an example of what Asif Agha (2007) calls a linguistic or semiotic *register* – a way of speaking or writing that is linked to stereotypical social personae, including their purported values, activities, behaviors, and so forth. These associations and meanings are learned as a part of socialization more broadly, as people acquire knowledge and understanding of the worlds in which they live, and they are a big part of why *how* something is said may be just as important as *what* is said, in Norway and elsewhere.

Registers are also the products of *enregisterment*, the sociohistorical process through which they develop over time through increasing awareness and circulation of language-personae links in discourse, including everyday talk but also media representations of various sorts (Agha 2007, 2011). The Norwegian dialect popularity contest of 2005, discussed in detail in Chapter 1, as well as kitchen-table discussions and secondary media coverage of the contest, are all excellent illustrations of dialect enregisterment as an ongoing process. That Norwegians are able to identify so many non-normative regional and local dialects by name and have strong feelings about them is evidence of dialect enregisterment in Norway and the extent to which *place* is a central component of social identity and social meaning-making there (cf. Maehlum and Hårstad 2018). Drawing on the work of semiotician C.S. Peirce, linguistic anthropologists also describe the relationship between regional dialect features and their place of origin as an *indexical* one. Valdresmål is a product and an *index* of Valdres; in social life, the dialect represents and points back (like an index finger) to the place and people from which it originates. As an enregistered dialect, Valdresmål not only represents Valdres and its residents, which is an example of *direct* or *first-order* indexicality (Silverstein 2003); it also represents the supposed qualities of that place and group of people (e.g., folksy, trustworthy), through *indirect* or *second-order* indexicality.

Like Valdresmål, most of Norway's distinctive regional ways of speaking are enregistered; however, quick indexical associations among language, place, and particular people or social personae are harder to come by for the more normative ways of speaking found in urban Eastern Norway, in and around the capital city of Oslo. This does not mean that Oslo and other nearby cities lack regional linguistic distinctions; rather, their de facto "standard" speech patterns (Mæhlum 2009) are not enregistered – or stereotyped – to nearly the same degree (cf. Røyneland 2020). In 2004, the year before the dialect popularity contest and several years before I started formal ethnographic research in Valdres, I was gathering data for my master's thesis on language in Norwegian broadcast media when I heard Oslo's relative lack of linguistic stereotypes articulated rather humorously in a radio series called *Språket Sladrer* (Language Gives You Away). Producers of the series had assembled a group of three young men, two from urban Eastern Norway and one from a small Western city, all nonexperts, who were there to discuss Norwegian dialects. They played a game of sorts, trying to one-up each other in naming famous Norwegians who spoke dialects from different places around the country, which went quickly and easily until Oslo came up.

(1) E1: *Er det noen som kjenner noen kjente folk som*
Does anyone know any famous people who
(2) *snakker Oslo dialekt, da?*
speak Oslo dialect, then?
(3) [group laughter]
(4) E2: *Nei faktisk – Nei den var verre altså –*
No actually – No that one is harder –
(5) W: *Ja, ja jeg føler meg litt sånn trist for e:, Østlendingene –*
Yeah, yeah I feel a little sad for um:, Easterners –
(6) *altså som e generaliserer det til, altså,*
who I'm generalizing this to, that is,
(7) *kor kommer de fra egentlig? Kem er det DE har?*
where are they actually from? Who do THEY have?
(8) *De har – de har liksom Bokmålsordboka, de.*
They have – they have like the Bokmål dictionary.
(9) *E:, de har ingen som gir*
Um:, they don't have anyone who gives [them]
(10) *sjel og – og saft og – og DIALEKT.*
soul and – and *saft* [lit. "juice" or "nectar"] and – and DIALECT.

In this playful metalinguistic conversation, Oslo is depicted as not having a dialect or any well-known, representative speakers, a situation the Western participant describes as "sad" in line 5 and further indicative of a lack of "soul and *saft*," as he says in line 10. Of course, linguistically speaking, Oslo and other urban Eastern places have their own regional features, but most of these are perceived as relatively unmarked most of the time and often less readily associated with stereotypical personae. Oslo speech features also seem to be less directly indexical of place (see Hilton 2010), which is partly tied to their use by nonlocals, particularly speakers from nearby towns and from rural and non-Eastern regions, whose marked dialects were historically stigmatized. In the twenty-first century, however, speaking a regional dialect has become socially desirable, indexing distinctive local places and identities and their positive interpretations in contemporary Norway. Today, dialects like Valdresmål can sound interesting, cool, soulful, and *saftig* (juicy), while "standard" Oslo speech is perceived as unmarked and unremarkable.

A consequence of the currently positive evaluation of marked regional dialects in Norway is that they are frequently heard in public and in relatively formal settings. Whereas in the US or the UK "standard" or "proper" English is generally expected in, for example, national news broadcasts or formal speeches, in Norway it is perfectly acceptable to use local and regional dialects in those contexts (Nesse 2015). At the same time, however, the widespread use of dialects like Valdresmål still does not mean that they are just "normal" or "natural" ways of speaking. On the contrary, as enregistered dialects with many layers of indexical meanings, they may be variously deployed as performances of place-based identity, for fun stylistic flair, or even to establish or reinforce an oppositional stance with nonlocals. The remainder of this chapter explores this kind of interactional multifunctionality for spoken Valdresmål, particularly in contexts where sociolinguists and anthropologists might expect to find speakers of marked dialects switching to more normative forms of speech, including appearances on national television and workplace encounters with "standard" speakers. Across such formal and public situations, many Valdres natives choose to use Valdresmål rather than shift toward a more normative register, and, in doing so, they take a pro-dialect stance, demonstrating an expectation that their interlocutors and audiences from elsewhere in Norway will understand what they say and be accepting of their dialect use.

SPEAKING VALDRESMÅL IN PUBLIC

Like code-switching among bilingual speakers, *style-shifting* – using more than one register or way of speaking within a single language – can indicate a change in the speech situation, such as a shift in the topic of conversation, audience, or setting, or it may serve a speaker's "metaphorical" or rhetorical purposes, among other things (Blom and Gumperz 1972; Bell 1984; Ervin-Tripp 2001; Hernández-Campoy and Cutillas-Espinosa 2012). The social multifunctionality of both code-switching and style-shifting has been well documented by sociolinguists and linguistic anthropologists in communities around the world, and switching or shifting toward "standard" or normative forms of speech in public and formal settings is an exceedingly common practice that contributes to the reproduction of sociolinguistic hierarchies in many places. In addition to understanding when and why speakers alternate between languages and styles, it is also important to pay attention to when and why people who are clearly capable of code-switching or style-shifting do *not* do those things. Stylistic consistency in the use of dialect, rather than style-shifting toward normative speech, is relatively common in Norway (Jahr and Janicki 1995; Kristiansen and Vikør 2006; Nesse 2015; Røyneland 2020), including for Valdresmål speakers, both in local contexts and when they find themselves in the media spotlight engaging with speakers of normative urban Eastern Norwegian or marked dialects from elsewhere in the country.

During the 2000s, quite a few teenaged and twenty-something Valdres natives achieved distinction at national and international levels in artistic performance and sports. Several of these young people became locally well-known for their use of relatively "broad" (*brei*) or "strong" Valdresmål in national media appearances, where they were often interviewed by speakers of unmarked or "standard" Eastern Norwegian. Despite the extremely public nature of these settings and their interviewers' normative speech patterns and positions of authority, many of Valdres's high-achieving youth made use of distinctive pronunciations, grammatical features, and unique words from Valdresmål in national media appearances.

Among these young local celebrities was Ingrid, a teenager who was recognized as something of a child musical prodigy and interviewed repeatedly by national news outlets as she qualified for a prestigious international competition for young musicians. In a live appearance on a national morning television program one day, Ingrid was interviewed by the program's two middle-aged cohosts, who made consistent use of normative urban Eastern speech patterns, perceptually close to standard written Bokmål. Ingrid, on the other hand, replied using marked Valdres dialect, sometimes in direct contrast to the hosts. For instance, in the short interview excerpt below, one of the hosts asked Ingrid about how things were going and used the normative form for the present participle "have/has been," *har vært* in line 1 (shown in bolded text), while Ingrid answered the host's questions using the Valdresmål form *ha vøre*, not just once but twice in lines 3 and 4 (also shown in bolded text).

(1) H: *Hvordan **har** de siste dagene **vært** da?*
So how have the last [few] days been?
(2) *Det er et ganske <u>travelt</u> program for deg?*
It's a pretty <u>busy</u> itinerary for you?
(3) I: *Det **ha vøre** ganske hektisk,*
It's been pretty hectic,
(4) *men det **ha** jo **vøre** utrule moro.*
but it has really been incredibly fun.

While the rest of Ingrid's response in lines 3–4 is basically *bivalent* (Woolard 1998), meaning all of the words and grammar "work" in both Valdresmål and Bokmål-esque speech, the contrast between *har vært* and *ha vøre* positions Ingrid as a marked dialect speaker in this brief exchange.

Contrasts like this are clear examples of *not* style-shifting in public media appearances, which was (and remains) quite common among Valdres residents making national headlines. In a similar example from the sporting world, Sigrunn, a university student and elite athlete from Valdres, also found herself in the media spotlight as she quickly rose through the international rankings in skiing. Throughout the course of an exciting and surprisingly successful season in the late 2000s, Sigrunn was interviewed by major national news outlets before and after each of her international competitions for Team Norway, and she made consistent use of Valdresmål in those media appearances, often in stark contrast to the normative Norwegian used by many journalists. For instance, in the following excerpt from a recorded post-race interview broadcast on the national evening news, Sigrunn replied to a reporter's question containing the normative form *fornøyd* (satisfied, pleased) in line 1 (shown in bold), which contrasted with Sigrunn's use of the marked form *fornøygd* in her answer in line 2.

(1) R: *Hvor **fornøyd** er du med fjerde plass?*
How satisfied are you with fourth place?
(2) S: *Jau. Det e e: ganske gøtt **fornøygd** med.*
Yeah. I:'m pretty well satisfied with it.
(3) *Det **e** nå iallfall **bære** enn e:m forrige gong då.*
It's at least better than u:m last time anyway.
(4) *Så: **mø** hadde jo pallen inna rekkevidde så:*
So: we had the [medalists'] platform in sight so:

The marked dialectal quality of Sigrunn's reply was also amplified by her use of the Valdresmål first-person pronouns *e* (I) (*jeg* in Bokmål and Oslo speech) in line 2 and *mø* (we) (*vi* in Bokmål and Oslo speech) in line 4, as well as the the r-less present-tense form of "be" (also *e*, but with a short vowel length) in line 2. Additionally, she uses non-normative phonology in *bære* (better) (normatively *bedre*) in line 3 and *gøtt* (good, well) in line 2 (normatively *godt*), the last of which is regularly described by Valdresmål speakers as an indispensable and immediately recognizable Valdres dialect word. The rest of Sigrunn's answer in this brief excerpt is also thoroughly dialectal, or at least bivalent with common Eastern forms, in terms of morphology and phonology, as were her other responses throughout this interview and many others.

Sigrunn's use of Valdresmål on-air was stylistically consistent with the ways I heard her speak in less public local contexts, and she was acutely aware of the fact that, for every media appearance, viewers back home were listening carefully not just to what she said but how she said it. After her breakthrough season had come to a close, I was able to talk with Sigrunn back in Valdres about speaking dialect in media interviews, and she told me that she had received many compliments on her use of Valdresmål from both friends and strangers.

(1) T: *Har du fått mykjy kommentara*
Have you gotten a lot of comments

(2) *om att du bruka dialekt i media?*
about using dialect in the media?

(3) S: *Ja::, det har e fått ein del komentara på.*
Yeah::, I've gotten quite a few comments about it.

(4) T: *Ja?*
Yeah?

(5) S: *<u>Positive</u> kommentara.*
<u>Positive</u> comments.

(6) T: *Berre positive?*
Just positive?

(7) S: *Ja, det ha vøre berre positivt. Det har det.*
Yeah, it's just been positive. It has.

(8) *Og det er jo særle følk i frå Valdres, då,*
And it's especially people from Valdres,

(9) *som seia at å dei syns det e så moro å høyra*
who say that oh they think it's so fun to hear

(10) *valdresdialekte på tv'en. @@ Og slekt då.*
the Valdres dialect on tv. @@ And things like that.

(11) T: *Mm-mm.*
Mm-hm.

(12) S: *Som syns det e veldi flott.*
Who think it's really nice.

(13) *Og:: men med andre, ja, journalista og,*
A::nd but others too, yeah, journalists and,

(14) *følk utanfrå med. Som em som seie det at*
people from outside too. Who um say that

(15) *dei syns det e flott at e held på dialekta, ja.*
they think it's nice that I keep up the dialect, yeah.

(16) *Og at e bruka den . i media.*
And that I use it . in the media.

(17) T: *Mm-mm.*
Mm-hm.

(18) S: *Mm-mm. Så det e:: jo veldi artigt å få*
Mm-hm. So it's:: of course really fun to get

(19) *positive kommentara på det. Mm-mm,*
positive comments about it. Mm-hm,

(20) *det gjere jo at e bli endå meir bevisst kanskje med på::*
that makes it so I get even more conscious maybe too of::

(21) *å fortsette med det og halde på dialekte.*
keeping it up and maintaining the dialect.

As Sigrunn says, people from Valdres and journalists alike made positive comments about the fact that she spoke Valdresmål in front of the news cameras. The unrelenting attention also made her more consciously aware of her own dialect use and contributed to her stylistic consistency.

Like Sigrunn, other Valdres natives who frequently appeared in mass media (athletes, musicians, and other performers, as well as local and regional news reporters) told me that they received only positive comments from Valdres residents and others about their public dialect use. In ethnographic and metalinguistic interviews with Valdres residents from all walks of life, people also often pointed out to me specific young, local celebrities whose dialect use they found to be impressive in media appearances. Both younger and older people told me how wonderful they thought it was to hear young people from Valdres using Valdresmål on television and on the radio. Sigrunn and Ingrid were among those who received such praise, as were several other well-known Valdres natives in their teens and twenties in the first decade of the twenty-first century. This kind of audience evaluation became personal, too, when some of the older people I spoke to praised my own use of Valdresmål in local and regional radio interviews regarding my research. I was flattered, but I also often worried that I was not speaking dialect well enough, mixing in too many Bokmål forms when I struggled to find (or simply did not know) the "correct" way to say things in Valdresmål.

Perhaps not surprisingly, then, some people I talked to also pointed out examples of media appearances by people from Valdres who they felt did *not* make adequate use of the dialect in the media spotlight (and thus failed to represent the district well), with little understanding or sympathy for style-shifting toward urban Eastern speech norms. I got to hear the other side of that kind of story, too: in a long interview I had with Kari, a Valdres native who had lived in Oslo for more than a decade before eventually moving back home, she related to me the experience of being the target of such negative attention. Following a brief appearance on a television game show, Kari told me that when she watched the playback she was surprised to hear how standard-sounding her speech was, and also that she had received negative comments from people back home in Valdres after the show aired.

> *Da va det ikkji særlig mykji Vallers dialekt e prata altså. Da hørte e det sjøl […] Da fekk e ein del kjeft etterpå tå følk uppi her da. "Herregud ko DU e ifrå då?"*

> I didn't speak very much Valdres dialect [on air]. Then I heard it myself […] Then I got a lot of flak afterward from people up here [in Valdres]. "Oh my god where are YOU from?"

While Kari self-identifies as a Valdresmål speaker and used many locally distinctive sounds and grammatical features in our conversations together (including many in the excerpt above, listed in Table 3.1), this piece of our interview also shows something of a contrast between Kari's own dialectal speech and her recollection of other Valdresmål speakers' negative comments. The question she remembers people asking, *Ko DU e ifrå?* (Where are YOU from?) contains a marked and decidedly "broad" dialect feature in the noninverted syntactic (word-order) pattern, where the verb *e* (are) is not shifted to the second position following the question word *ko* (where) as it would be in normative syntax, like Bokmål *Hvor er du fra?* (The equivalent in English would be normative "Where are you from?" compared to non-normative "Where you are from?").

The noninverted Valdresmål syntactic pattern stands out as "broader," or more highly marked, than most of the other dialect features Kari uses, and it is therefore a useful example of the highly variable nature of dialect use and how, in practice, "dialect" and "standard" exist on something of a stylistic continuum, rather than as well-defined and delimited varieties. While Kari herself uses many common Valdresmål words and pronunciations (see Table 3.1), the syntax in *Ko DU e ifrå?* implies that those who criticized her on-air speech were likely speakers of more "broad" Vallers, also known for taking more staunch positions about the relationship between consistent dialect use and loyalty to the local community. This example also shows just how important it is for many Norwegians to be able to identify where someone is from based on their language, echoing the *Språket Sladrer* radio conversation mentioned earlier, in which the West-Norwegian participant said he felt sad for Easterners because, as he put it, "Where are they actually from?" when they do not speak in a way that easily locates them in geographic space.

As we talked about Kari's game show experience and other times she recalled noticing herself unintentionally style-shifting toward normative speech patterns, Kari also acknowledged that she uses less marked dialect around people from outside of Valdres fairly often. But, she explained, "it's not like I want to hide that I'm from Valdres. It's just that, ugh, it [Bokmål] slips in so quickly." She attributed her inadvertent style-shifting to having gone to university, lived, and worked in the heart of Oslo in the 1980s and 1990s, and to the stigma and stereotypes she felt as a Valdresmål speaker there at the time, a not-uncommon situation for speakers of marked dialects from elsewhere in Norway, too (Sollid 2014).

Table 3.1. Non-normative Valdresmål forms in Kari's interview excerpt, compared to those most common in Bokmål and normative Eastern speech

Valdresmål	Bokmål and normative Eastern speech	English gloss
va	*var*	was
ikkji	*ikke*	not
mykji	*mye*	much
e	*jeg*	I
prata	*snakket*	spoke
sjøl	*selv*	self
fekk	*fikk*	got
tå	*av*	from
følk	*folk*	people
uppi her	*her oppe*	up here

Today, however, many Valdresmål speakers consciously choose not to moderate the distinctiveness of their dialect in public or in other interactions with more standard speakers. Instead, they seem to be using the Valdres dialect to perform a desirably distinctive and *saftig* (juicy), place-based, rural identity, as well as to satisfy the local audience back home in Valdres, where there is clearly social pressure to represent Valdres well by speaking dialect in national media appearances. In this interplay between habitual speech patterns and individual intentions, on the one hand, and social expectations for public language use, on the other, we see some of the complex mechanics involved in the continuous, ongoing process of enregisterment for Valdresmål.

STYLE AND STEREOTYPES IN MASS MEDIA

Understanding Valdresmål as not just a dialect but also a register allows us to think about it as an important element in the production of "style" beyond language, which anthropologists often define in terms of distinctiveness and differentiation within a lived system of social meanings (Bourdieu 1991; Mendoza-Denton 1999; Gal and Irvine 2019). Language is one among potentially very many meaningful signs and practices comprising and differentiating any particular style, which always "exists only in relation to agents endowed with schemes of perception and appreciation that enable them to constitute it as a set of systematic differences" (Bourdieu 1991, 39). Style, linguistic and otherwise, is thus about both production and perception, so that stylistic distinction cannot be generated by an individual speaker alone. Instead, a necessary component in the achievement of style is its broader recognition, the shared perception and interpretation by people taking in the message.

This brings us back to the many ways in which language ideologies are central to social life, including in mediatized contexts. Journalists and producers in Norway's national news and entertainment media often pay explicit attention to program participants' and interviewees' use of marked dialects. They comment directly on, react to, and sometimes even appropriate distinctive dialect forms, all of which points back to the larger stylistic and linguistic-semiotic system at hand. It is not unusual for journalists and program hosts to make positive mention of the distinctiveness of a guest or interviewee's dialect on air, as in the following example, taken from near the end of one of Ingrid's extended live-television interviews in the lead-up to her international music competition.

(1) H: *Vi hører jo på den flotte dialekten din [at eh du –*
We hear in your beautiful dialect [that uh you –
(2) I: *[@@*
(3) H: *Ja, de som er veldig godt kjent da –*
Yes, [for] those who are very well acquainted then –
(4) *Aurdal. Det er altså da en fjellbygd i <u>Valdres</u>.*
Aurdal. That's a mountain village in <u>Valdres</u>.
(5) *Er det mange som eh – som gjør det samme som du*
Are there many who uh – who do the same as you
(6) I: *[@@*
(7) H: *[velger og ha:r, ja:, forelsket seg fullstendigt*
[choose and ha:ve, yeah:, fallen completely in love
(8) *i et instrument?*
with an instrument?
(9) I: *Det e mange som spele: hardingfele og*
There are a lot who play: Hardanger fiddle
(10) *følkemusikk då – det e stort miljø for det.*
and folk music – there's a big scene for that.

In line 1 of this excerpt, one of the program hosts first compliments Ingrid on her use of Valdresmål, which she laughs off in line 2, not responding further. Then the host plays on the popular Norwegian pastime of identifying the geographic origin of her dialect down to the microlocal level, which he misidentifies as a mountain village in line 4. (In fact, it is a sizable town along the main highway at the base of the central Valdres valley.) In lines 5 and 7–8, the host asks Ingrid whether other people in Valdres have a similar love for instruments, implicitly connecting Valdres and Valdresmål to music. Ingrid takes this up as meaning traditional folk music in lines 9–10, something that is popularly associated with rural culture and language in the larger semiotic system. This brief exchange is another prime example of the kinds of discourse that underlie processes of (re-)enregisterment, linking speakers and linguistic registers to places, activities, and the larger sociocultural world (Agha 2007).

In other instances, the attention paid to marked dialect use is less explicit, but "positive" stereotypes of Valdres and Valdresmål speakers are made salient in other ways. After one of Sigrunn's big ski races, for example, a national evening sports news broadcast replayed this soundbite from her pre-race interview:

På syndag så går e: jaktstart i Ruhpolding. Og håpa å vinne. @

On Sunday I:'m racing pursuit in Ruhpolding. And [I] hope to win. @

In the post-race news broadcast, Sigrunn's cheeky articulation of an ambitious pre-race goal, delivered in marked Valdresmål, was immediately juxtaposed with the NRK sportscaster's in-studio commentary, delivered in normative Eastern Norwegian and, by contrast, quite dryly:

@ *Ja, det sa hun før jaktstarten, og SELVFØLGELIG vant hun når hun hadde sagt det, for jenter fra Valdres er ALLTID å stole på. Vi gratulerer.*

@ Yes, she said that before the pursuit race, and OF COURSE she won once she had said it, because you can ALWAYS trust a girl from Valdres. We say congratulations.

Together, the linguistic and stylistic contrasts and the commentary itself worked to invoke and reinforce enduring sociolinguistic stereotypes.

The pre-race interview soundbite had already been played countless times on NRK that day, both before and after the race, as the significance of the message (Sigrunn's "plan" to win) grew throughout the competition, where she did eventually come in first. Just as other sportscasters had done in earlier broadcasts, the evening news sports host quoted above connected the "truth" of Sigrunn's "prediction" of a win to the supposed trustworthiness of Valdres residents and Valdresmål speakers. The underlying message about language may be left relatively implicit in this case, but media comments like these evoke dominant language ideologies linking marked-dialect speakers to particular sociocultural values and personae (Agha 2007; Irvine and Gal 2000). In the sense that only "positive" stereotypes are alluded to here for Valdres and Valdresmål, they are effectively elevated within the Norwegian dialect hierarchy, while being simultaneously reconstrained to certain social and cultural domains, like folk music and rural, trust-based communities.

These kinds of dialect-related stereotypes are often deployed in humorous or otherwise lighthearted contexts (see Swinehart 2008), but they also pop up in other, more directly problematic ways. Kari, who faced criticism after *not* speaking Valdresmål on television, told me she felt these constraints acutely during her young adulthood in Oslo, where she routinely ran into stereotypes associated with speaking dialect in general and Valdresmål in particular. For Kari, the problem of dialect-stereotyping led her to sometimes consciously style-shift when interacting with city folk at work and in social settings:

> *For at e bi tatt meir seriøst nokon gonge, når e gjør det. Og så føle e og at mange gonge så blir du veldig fort satt i eit slags bås da, når du prata dialekt.* [...] *Når du høyre at du er fra Valdres så "å ja da ko trur du om nynorskens framtid og du er veldig opptatt av DET sikkert. Og at du da sikkert driv med – ja, er bonde da, og at du sikkert e flink med følkedans og sånn."*
>
> Because I'm taken more seriously sometimes, when I do [shift toward Bokmål]. And I also feel that many times you're very

> quickly like put in a box, when you speak dialect. […] When you hear that you're from Valdres, it's like "oh yeah what do you think about the future of Nynorsk and you're probably very interested in THAT. And that you probably do – yeah, are like a farmer, and that you're probably good at folk dancing and things like that."

While stigma attached to speaking dialect in public and in urban contexts seems to have waned considerably in the decades since Kari moved back to Valdres, many of the same old stereotypes continue to circulate, not only in face-to-face interaction but also via playful, innocuous-sounding comments in mass media, like those celebrating Sigrunn and her athletic accomplishments or Ingrid and her love of music.

We have already seen that Valdres residents themselves pay a lot of attention to the use of Valdresmål on radio and television, and from the above examples it is clear that Norwegian journalists and producers also take up and play on the style and stereotypes associated with marked dialects, both in interviews and in editing and other production decisions. Observing the historic unfolding of processes of sociolinguistic valorization, Agha has argued that an accumulation of many successive meaning-generating utterances and events is required (2007, 228). Most of these may happen in everyday contexts, but in a thoroughly mediatized world, like that of twenty-first-century Norway, technology and broadcast media can play a considerable role. As Jane Hill has also pointed out, because of the ways in which everyday life today is "utterly saturated with talk and text from media, … media language must count as yet another form of 'everyday language'" (2008, vii). For the case of Valdresmål, there is a self-reinforcing quality to stylistic choices involving incredibly public uses of dialect in national broadcast media, and we underestimate its significance at risk to our understandings of more "everyday" kinds of linguistic practice. Effective interpretation of more ordinary, less public uses of language requires contextualization within the contemporary, media-oriented social world, as well as within the long-term history of sociolinguistic conflict and differentiation in Norway discussed in Chapter 2. What happens linguistically face-to-face and in real-time is at once a product of sociolinguistic history and tangled up with contemporary linguistic and stylistic trends generated in mediatized social life.

EVERYDAY RESISTANCE IN LOCAL INTERACTIONS

Returning to the local context, Valdres dialect speakers also interact with people from outside the district in lots of situations closer to home. Particularly in the booming tourism and recreation industry, Valdres locals find themselves frequently needing to converse with visitors and cabin owners from more urban settings, who often use quite normative spoken Norwegian. Many Valdres workplaces are thus active sites for linguistic engagement and differentiation with nonlocals, including, most obviously, retail shops and businesses in the hospitality sector, like restaurants, hotels, and campgrounds, but also in less obvious places, like the construction and home-services industries, which are responsible for the building and maintenance of Valdres's thousands and thousands of vacation cabins.

The frequency and intensity of engagement with outsiders has increased as tourism development has ramped up over the last decade or two, but encounters with urban visitors are nothing new. For more than a century, Valdres has seen seasonal influxes of city folk seeking time outdoors in the countryside and surrounding mountains during the summer months and cross-country skiing from mountain cabins or lodges in the winter and early spring. Valdres's position along a main arterial highway linking Oslo and Bergen has also brought countless passersby to the district over generations. So there is plenty of precedent for interacting with people who do not speak Valdresmål, and, while those interactions are usually unremarkable, locals also often reflect on times when language and sociolinguistic differentiation have risen to the surface and complicated the situation.

Eva, an elderly Nynorsk and dialect activist, told me that the problem of mutual intelligibility was a common one when she worked as a receptionist in the 1950s and 1960s. Urban visitors often called or stopped by the shop, she said, and, while she never had trouble understanding their relatively standard speech, it was not unusual that they failed to understand everything she said in Valdresmål. In those instances, as the speaker of a marked dialect, the responsibility for comprehension and conversational repair fell squarely to Eva, who obliged but not necessarily with compassion:

Det hende n laut overseta einkort ord då, veit du, viss det kom nokon so va før dum.

Sometimes you had to translate a few words, you know, if someone [nonlocal] came in who was too stupid.

According to Eva, because they did not always understand what Valdresmål speakers said or meant, urban outsiders were plainly stupid. This kind of matter-of-fact judgment was and is common, and I have heard it articulated especially frequently by Valdres locals working in retail, service, and tourism-adjacent industries.

Stian, a high school student and stage performer, worked part-time at a grocery store near the main highway in the late 2000s and shared a similar perspective. In a metalinguistic interview focused on dialect and how he used it at home, at school, with friends, and at work, we shared a laugh as he walked me through a common grocery store encounter as a dialect-speaking cashier serving many customers from outside the district.

(1) T: *Bruke du dialekt heile tie når du e på jobb?*
Do you always use dialect when you're at work?
(2) S: *Ja ja. Det e jo mange som – spesielt dette me*
Yeah, yeah. There's a lot of people who – like especially
(3) *viss du spør om dei ska ha ei <u>pøse</u> då?*
if you ask if they want a <u>bag</u> [*pøse*]?
(4) T: *Mm-mm.*
Mm-hm.
(5) S: *Så e det mange so e veit dei forstår det*
Then there's a lot of people who I know understand
(6) *så heilt GARANTERT ko e meina for noko, men det e berre for*
completely GUARANTEED, what I mean, but just to
(7) *å vera vrang, så *hva*? Men då. Då bi e så sur @@*
be difficult [they say] *What*? But then. Then I get crabby @@
(8) *så då bi det, JA SKA DU HA EI PØSE? *HVA?**
so it turns into, YEAH DO YOU WANT A *PØSE*? *WHAT?*
(9) *PØSE. [*HVA?* <u>PØSE!</u>*
PØSE. [*What?* <u>*PØSE*!</u>

(10) T: [@@@

(11) S: *Te slutt så forstår dei det då. Når dei ha stått der*
Eventually they understand it. When they've stood there

(12) *og hakka det ut.*
and thought it through.

(13) T: *Men du nekte å si pose?* @
But you refuse to say *pose*? @

(14) S: @ *Ja, e gjere det. For at* – @ *E kunne sikkert sagt det,*
@ Yeah, I do. Because – @ I could totally say that,

(15) *men at det e så irriterande når at dei liksom ikkji ska forstå*
but it's so irritating when they like don't want to understand

(16) @ *ko e meina for noko. For det GJERE dei jo.*
@ what I mean. Because of course they DO.

(17) T: *Mm-mm.*
Mm-hm.

(18) S: *Det e kji SÅ vanskelig visst n tenkje se litt um.*
It's not SO hard if you just think about it a little.

An interesting feature of Stian's story here is that he uses an imagined, hypothetical "city-person voice," indicated by surrounding asterisks in lines 7–9 above, which stands in clear contrast to Stian's own use of fairly broad Valdresmål. *Hva*, used in lines 7–9, is the normative form of "what," used in written Bokmål and urban Eastern speech, while Stian, in his own voice within our interaction, uses the Valdresmål form *ko* in lines 6 and 16. Stian's use of *hva* in lines 7–9 is an excellent example of *multivocality*, the layering of multiple voices, real or imagined, in narrated dialogue (Bakhtin 1981; Hill 1995; Wroblewski 2021), as he uses his own (literal) voice to also narrate what urban customers have said or would say.

The focal contrast in Stian's story, though, is the vowel difference in local and normative forms of the word for "bag": *pøse* (in lines 3, 8, and 9) versus *pose* (line 13). In purely linguistic terms, this is a minor difference: the normative vowel is /o/, which contrasts with the /ø/ vowel used in Valdresmål, while the rest of the sounds in the word are the same. To compare this to an example from US English, the *pøse-pose* contrast is similar to variable regional pronunciations of "roof," where the vowel sound may be either /u/ or /ʊ/; however, the /ø/-for-/o/ pattern in Valdresmål occurs more frequently and is a particularly salient and distinctive feature of local phonology (i.e., the systematic patterning of sounds). In Stian's narrative, the minor linguistic difference in *pøse* and *pose* leads to a major communicative breakdown, as the city-person customer asks Stian *Hva?* (What?) over and over again, repeatedly failing to understand that *pøse* refers to the same thing that they call *pose* (lines 7–9). For Stian, it is not just a matter of referential meaning (i.e., dictionary definition), though, because he interprets the customer's failure to understand as being intentionally difficult (lines 5–7), willfully ignorant (lines 15–16), and not making enough effort to think it through (line 18). The social-indexical contrasts and meanings of *pøse* and *pose* are far more important than the linguistic and referential ones, as Stian's playful account of an everyday sociolinguistic struggle invokes enduring, power-laden oppositions between rural and urban language and people.

Stian's narrative and surrounding commentary demonstrate that, in addition to representing a local identity and positively-valued, distinctive style, speaking Valdresmål with outsiders can also function as a means of resistance to outside imposition, linguistic and perhaps otherwise. In general, using the local dialect in an interaction with a normative-sounding city person, as Stian and many others report doing, might index self-consciously pro-dialect or pro-Valdres ideologies. However, over the course of the interaction narrated by Stian above, brief and hypothetical as it may be, using Valdresmål also comes to represent an oppositional stance toward the city person, who Stian is sure is capable of understanding that *pøse* means "bag." There is an implied expectation in the customer's repeated question (*Hva?*) that Stian should shift to a more normative way of speaking to accommodate their lack of immediate comprehension. But Stian openly resists by repeating the dialect form *pøse* more loudly and more deliberately each time, rather than just saying *pose*, even though he is well aware of the normative pronunciation and could easily articulate it. As the narrated speech event unfolds, it becomes clear that the problem, for Stian, is not a linguistic one but a matter of local and personal pride. Why should he have to take responsibility for the customer's failure to understand? Why should it be acceptable for urban outsiders to not only be ignorant of rural language but also not demonstrate any effort to make sense of the unfamiliar pronunciation of a word that is common in retail transactions everywhere?

Stian's story is particular to the linguistic and social dynamics in Valdres and in Norway, but similar encounters with sociolinguistic inequality play out in so many other places where historically marginalized and linguistically minoritized speakers are expected to bear more than their fair share of the communicative burden. Sometimes, as for Kari, it takes the form of style-shifting toward normative speech from the outset to avoid, as much as possible, the chance of misunderstanding or linguistic stereotyping and discrimination. Other times, as in Eva's and Stian's experiences, speakers of marked, nonstandard ways of speaking might be asked or even required to explain themselves by "translating" for the benefit of those whose habitual ways of speaking are more closely aligned with standard or normative patterns. The weaponization of linguistic difference in the service of claiming sociolinguistic privilege is pervasive and difficult to disrupt, and resistance can take many forms, from overt linguistic-political activism to the mundane stubbornness of refusing to translate a single word that, as Stian says, is not "SO hard if you just think about it a little" (line 18).

So what does it mean to speak Valdresmål in public or in other interactions with nonlocal speakers? In some cases it may be an on-trend bit of stylistic distinction, a way to sound cool and interesting and stand out from the crowd. In other situations, it may be a way to enthusiastically signal local pride while simultaneously satisfying the expectations of people back home – and knowing the potential social costs of not sounding Valdres enough. At certain times, it may be used to take up a pro-local stance, resisting long-term sociolinguistic inequalities, even in ordinary, passing encounters. Why, when, and how people use Valdresmål depends on so many layers of context, some general and some unique, often in tension with one another: the long history of language planning and politics, the specific person one is talking to, who might be listening or even just potentially overhear, being in a forgiving mood or a surly one, the foreseeable consequences of being taken seriously or pigeonholed in the moment. All of these things and so many more can matter, as they do for ways of speaking perceived as nonstandard in countless other places and communities. Like dialect itself, the meanings and relationships its use generates are variable, positioned, and emergent in interaction.

CHAPTER FOUR

Pro-dialect Ideology and the Dynamics of Language Change

As long as they are actively spoken, all languages and language varieties are always changing, both in terms of social meaning and linguistic structure, and ideologies of language can certainly play a role in structural change (Labov 1963; Woolard 2008; Holmes and Kerswill 2008). Yet, as linguistic anthropologist Kathryn Woolard (2008) has noted, most research examining language ideologies over the past several decades "has focused on the reciprocal links between linguistic ideologies and social relations. The links between linguistic ideologies and linguistic forms, and particularly the effects of the former on the latter, have been relatively slighted" (436). In the preceding chapters, we have already seen how language ideologies influence sociolinguistic perception and interaction for Valdresmål speakers, but it is also the case that ideologies of language, especially pro-dialect ideologies, appear to positively affect the retention of certain Valdresmål features and novel directions of change for others, a few of which I will discuss in detail in this chapter.

Nevertheless, and despite recent dialect revalorization in Valdres, a much longer-term trend in local language change has been movement toward regionally dominant, normative features. In the 1990s, dialect use among youth in Valdres was clearly on the decline, with strong evidence of change in the direction of Oslo speech patterns among teenagers (Kvåle 1999), as many young people in Valdres aspired to a more "modern," urban life in the middle and late twentieth century.

In addition, many ultra-local linguistic forms – those associated with particular villages in the Valdres valley – have long ago fallen out of regular use (Beito 1959; Kvåle 1999), as residents became increasingly mobile over the course of the twentieth century, both within Valdres and beyond. Among the sociolinguistic effects of geographic mobility is that children often have parents from different places and are therefore exposed to multiple ways of speaking Norwegian from their earliest years, which contributes to less use of highly distinctive or unusual features (cf. Sandøy 2015). This kind of loss has given way to a more uniform way of speaking in the central part of the main Valdres valley through what sociolinguists call *dialect leveling* or *convergence*, a process by which nearby dialects may lose some of the features that made them slightly different from one another while retaining other shared, but still marked, local forms. Dialect leveling is a well-documented pattern elsewhere in Norway and in other European contexts, as well (Kerswill 2003; Røyneland 2005; Auer et al. 2005).

In addition to internal dialect leveling in Valdresmål, long-term dialect shift or convergence toward urban, regional norms also continues. Working within a framework that insists we consider the sociopolitical meaningfulness of language contact and change, literary theorist and philosopher of language Mikhail Bakhtin conceptualizes different varieties of language as exerting centripetal and centrifugal forces in social life (1981). For Bakhtin, standard or normative forms of language have strong unifying tendencies and centripetal force, contributing to the consolidation of social and linguistic power and authority. At the same time, less normative linguistic forms always exist, and their persistence necessarily counters the power of "unitary" language with centrifugal, disunifying force, pulling away from the relatively solid, stable center. As discussed in previous chapters, there is no single, authoritative form of Norwegian; instead, there are two written norms, Bokmål and Nynorsk, and no widely recognized spoken standard, though urban, Eastern speech patterns can be regarded as normative. Additionally, distinctive local dialects have generally high social value and symbolic importance today, which is indexical of alternative sources of authority. While Bakhtin's model does not directly address the complexity of this situation, I find it useful to think of each linguistic norm or enregistered variety (see Chapter 3) as having its own centripetal force, which can also work centrifugally against the others, similar to the multiple gravitational fields operating in a single solar system. In this case, Bokmål, Nynorsk, Oslo speech, and Valdresmål (among other dialects) are all spinning fast enough to have a core that sticks together, but smaller, less normative varieties like Valdresmål are also pulled toward those with stronger gravitational fields, which have grown and developed over centuries through widespread use in literature, media, and education, among other places.

The undeniable, long-term patterns of dialect convergence have meant the loss of some of Valdres's most unique linguistic features, along with the social and geographic differentiation they once represented, and this has been a source of frustration and grief for many in Valdres since the late twentieth century. As discussed in Chapter 1, it is not unusual to hear middle-aged and older people lament that contemporary Valdresmål is "watered down" or even on the verge of being lost completely, with blame readily cast on young people, who have long led processes of local leveling and convergence toward regionally normative urban forms. Dialect purism, including a belief that youth no longer speak "proper" Valdresmål, continues to circulate widely, but teens and young adults in contemporary Valdres nevertheless still identify as dialect speakers. Moreover, most young people are eager to keep Valdresmål and other Norwegian dialects alive, to keep them spinning, even as they are pulled on by the forces of more normative language. When I sat down for an extended interview with Eivind, one of the youths involved in producing the celebratory "We Beat the Hallingdalers!" banner after Valdres won the dialect popularity contest (discussed in Chapter 1), I asked about this directly.

T: *Det e jo mange, kanskje i besteforeldre generasjonen nå som vilde påstå at dei unge ikkji bruke dialekt lenger. Em, men du – altså e høre at du bruke den og det e mange e ha prata med so bruke den. Men, em, ko syns du om det? Trur du at det e sant, enn?*

There are a lot of people, maybe in the grandparent generation now who would claim that the young people don't use dialect anymore. Um, but you – like I hear that you're using it and lots of people I've talked to use it. But, um, what do you think about that? Do you think it's true, or?

E: *Både og. Det tru e går veldi opp og ned. Em, det e egentle litt sånn som mykjy anna e basert på trende. Fordi at em. Du ska ·kke så* <u>*mange*</u> *år tebake før det å bruke dialekt på ein måte va skikkele – skikkele* <u>*ut*</u>. *Mens dei siste åra, og spesielt – for vår del å ha sett at dialekta vår vann kåringe, og det ha vøre mykji bra fokus på dialektbruk, ha det vørte veldig trendy att å halde på. Og det e mø jo veldig glad før, og det håpe e selvfølgele at også ska bestå framover. For det e jo – fryktele synd visst dialektlandskapet i norge generelt blir burte.*

Yes and no. I think it really goes up and down. Um, it's actually like a lot of other things based on trends. Because um. You don't have to go back <u>many</u> years before using dialect in a way was really – really <u>out</u>. But the last few years, and especially – for us to have seen that our dialect won the contest, and there's been a lot of positive focus on dialect use, it's become very trendy to keep it up. And we're really happy for that, and I hope of course that it will continue in the future. Because it's really – it's a terrible shame if the dialect landscape in Norway in general were to disappear.

Clearly, Eivind was motivated to continue using dialect, despite the common perception that Valdresmål was fading away, and he hoped to see dialect diversity maintained throughout the country. Eivind's desire for the future perseverance of the local dialect is shared by everyone I have talked to in Valdres, and this contemporary pro-dialect ideology seems to have shored up and strengthened certain Valdresmål features, interrupting the otherwise steady, long-term, convergence toward normative Eastern speech patterns.

In the remainder of this chapter, I turn to discussion and analysis of some specific linguistic forms, ranging from lexicon (words) to phonology (pronunciation), to assess what seemed stable in Valdresmål toward the end of the first decade of the 2000s, as well as what was changing and in which directions. To do this, I use an approach from sociolinguistics called *apparent-time* analysis, in which the speech of representative speakers from successive generations is collected at a single time point and compared, with the assumption that many of the differences across generational groups represent language change over time. So when we find elderly people speaking differently than teenagers, we can infer that language has changed over the course of the older speakers' lifetimes. Working primarily from recorded interviews in this case, an apparent-time approach gives us a snapshot of the extent to which the use of certain linguistic forms varied among self-identified Valdresmål speakers ranging in age from eighteen to eighty-one in the late 2000s. For some high-frequency features, I am able to present precise quantitative analysis, while others are assessed primarily qualitatively for several reasons: (1) not all features occur frequently enough in the space of an hour-long conversational interview to produce valid statistics; (2) the relative salience of some features as important to, or defining of, Valdresmål makes it likely that people will use them more often when talking with me *about* dialect; and (3) my own use of many Valdresmål features as an interviewer makes it more likely that my interviewees will use them, as well.

Below, I begin with some examples of steady, ongoing change toward regional urban norms for a small but representative group of features, though there are probably more than enough to fill this book. I then consider how pro-dialect ideologies may be contributing to the resilience of other Valdresmål features and perhaps leading to new changes in non-normative directions. Taken together, these patterns show that contemporary dialect change in Valdres is complex and multidirectional, the result of presently strong centripetal sociolinguistic forces for multiple varieties of Norwegian, which simultaneously reinforce local distinctiveness for some features and contribute to ongoing convergence toward more normative patterns for others.

LONG-TERM CHANGE AND NORMALIZATION

For generations, Valdresmål has been in direct contact with normative, urban Eastern speech patterns, as well as the nationally dominant Bokmål written norm. Normative Eastern Norwegian speech has had a regular presence in Valdres through, among other things, national radio and television broadcasts (beginning in the 1920s and 1950, respectively) and more than a century of seasonal tourism, while Bokmål has long dominated national print media, so that reading everything from newspapers to novels and now digital resources most often exposes readers to Bokmål words and grammar. Large numbers of Valdres residents have also moved out of the district, most readily to nearby Eastern cities, including Oslo, for secondary and higher education and for work. Whether returning to Valdres for short visits or moving back permanently, Valdres out-migrants often bring more normative speech patterns back home with them. All of these things have contributed to long-term convergence toward urban Eastern speech norms, as have recent economic shifts away from small-scale farming and toward recreational and cultural tourism. The examples of long-term convergence that follow show the effects of the strong centripetal forces exerted by dominant forms of Norwegian and the social and economic power they represent.

Lexical Shift

When I talk with people in Valdres about dialect change, most are very aware of "old" Valdresmål words that have fallen out of regular use, if not entirely, at least among younger speakers, and this is of particular concern for many who are preoccupied with dialect loss. Unsurprisingly, some of the "traditional" Valdresmål words that are declining or no longer in everyday use refer to the tools and practices of manual agriculture and timber activities, which once constituted Valdres's economic base. As these industries have been increasingly mechanized, the words for many manual tools and activities are no longer regularly used, because they no longer have a place in people's day-to-day lives, only in historical accounts and reminiscences. Knowing such words today is a form of local history-keeping and trivia, but they have little practical value in an era of ever more automated cow-milking, hay-baling, and wood production.

Many other, less specialized words have also declined in use, yielding to the normalizing pressure of intensified social contact with urban speakers and more widely used linguistic forms. As long as fifty years ago, research on dialect use in Valdres concluded that many locally distinctive lexical items were on the decline, and that younger Valdres residents were essentially swapping in synonymous words from urban Eastern Norwegian speech and Bokmål instead (Wangensteen 1971). This trend continued through the late twentieth century, as documented in a sociolinguistic survey of teenagers and their parents in the 1990s

(Kvåle 1999), and it is still ongoing today. There are far more examples of lexical shift than could be examined in the space of this chapter or book, but an illustrative example is that of the Valdresmål general intensifying words *grådig* and *grepa*, both meaning "very/really/a lot," which have been largely displaced by normative *veldig* among younger speakers. For a comparison to North American English, we might consider this as similar to the Boston-area general intensifier "wicked," for which "very" or "really" can easily be substituted without changing the referential meaning. Of course, "wicked" has a more specific meaning in English outside of the Boston area; this is a further similarity, with *grådig* also found in both Bokmål and Nynorsk dictionaries but there meaning "greed(il)y," rather than being a general intensifier.

General intensifiers like *grådig*, *grepa*, and *veldig* are high-frequency lexical items, with at least one of these forms occurring multiple times in every interview recording I have, making this shift a relatively easy one to document. In my late 2000s recordings, most speakers under the age of fifty or so use *grådig* and/or *grepa* only infrequently, typically not more than a handful of times during an hour-long interview. In fact, while it has enough salience to have circulated in local marketing campaigns and business names over the last decade, *grepa* is quite uncommon in everyday use, even among the oldest Valdresmål speakers I recorded. On the other hand, *grådig* continues to be used regularly as a general intensifier by middle-aged and older speakers, as well as by some younger speakers who claim to be making a conscious effort to maintain Valdresmål in their speech. For instance, Ingebjørg, who was in her early twenties at the time, used *grådig* more than twice as often as she used *veldig* during the forty-two minutes of our interview recording, including three times in the space of sixteen seconds in this excerpt:

> *N såg jo det* ***grådigt*** *etter den dere konkuransa. Så vart det* ***grådigt*** *meir populært å prata dialekt. Særle blant ungdom. For att det e* <u>*dei*</u> *som på ein måte som ha vøre usikre på om det ha vøre kult. Og då* <u>*vart*</u> *det plutsele kult. Så e tru det va* ***grådigt*** *positivt for distriktet og for valdresdialekten faktisk, at dei vann.*
>
> You **really** saw that after that contest. Then it became **a lot** more popular to speak dialect. Especially among youth. Because <u>they're</u>

> the ones who have sort of been unsure about whether it was cool. And then it suddenly <u>became</u> cool. So I think it was **very** positive for the district and for the Valdres dialect actually, that they won.

Given that the topical focus at this point in the interview was the Valdres dialect, Ingebjørg's use of marked dialect features could easily be intensified, a common pattern in "self-conscious" speech, where speakers' attention is drawn to their active use of distinctive features (Schilling-Estes 1998). But I talked *about* dialect, *in* dialect, with all of the Valdresmål speakers I interviewed, and Ingebjørg was clearly different from others in her generation, with a social background that helps explain her outlier status. Raised on a family farm in central Valdres by parents who were raised on their families' farms in the same general area, Ingebjørg aspired to continue the local tradition of small-scale dairy farming. This has become more and more unusual for young people in Valdres today, as many have parents from different places and as farm kids witness their parents' struggles with needing to work at least part-time off the farm to make ends meet. While the latter was true for Ingebjørg, too, keeping up Valdres traditions of many sorts, including dialect, was still very important to her.

In addition, Ingebjørg's parents had been active in the local Mållag, a group that advocates for Nynorsk and dialect in the district and beyond, and they had explicitly encouraged their children to speak "proper" Valdresmål growing up. I asked about this, curious to hear more about the experience of having non-normative, dialectal speech "corrected" at home:

(1) T: *Det ha no vøre mykjy prat om språk heime hjå de med.*
So there's been a lot of talk about language at home too.

(2) I: @[@ ***<u>Grådigt</u>***. @@@
@[@ <u>A lot</u>. @@@

(3) T: [@@@

(4) *Ja, vart det retta på mykjy [i språket ditt?*
So were you corrected a lot [in your language?

(5) I: *[Ja.*
[Yes.

(6) *Mm-mm. Det hendte det. Treotjue år,*

Mm-hm. That's happened. Twenty-three years,
(7) *og kjem te å bi treotjue år i framtia. [@@*
and it'll be for twenty-three [more] years in the future. [@@
(8) T: [@@@
(9) I: *Og dei e* ***veldig*** *opptakne tå at e ska prata rettigt* [...]
And they're very concerned that I should speak correctly [...]

Laughing throughout our exchange, Ingebjørg had a sense of humor about having had her Valdresmål corrected by her parents over the course of her lifetime and foresaw it continuing "twenty-three more years in the future," as she says in lines 6–7. She also uses *grådigt* (a lot) again in line 2 of this excerpt when I try to prompt her to talk about how much her parents talked about language growing up. But even as a committed, self-conscious Valdresmål speaker, Ingebjørg is not categorical in her use of *grådig* and *grepa* – that is, she does not use them all of the time. In line 9, above, in an otherwise markedly dialectal sentence, Ingebjørg uses normative *veldig*, and over the duration of the interview recording, *veldig* accounts for about one third of the total occurrences of these three general intensifiers.

Nearly every other word in Ingebjørg's sentence in line 9 is aligned with Valdresmål, as was very often the case for uses of *veldig* among other dialect speakers I recorded, including in other quoted excerpts throughout this book. I therefore interpret this not just as an example of lexical shift from the distinctive Valdresmål forms *grådig* and *grepa* to normative *veldig* but also as evidence that, especially for younger speakers, *veldig* has effectively been incorporated into contemporary Valdresmål as a neutral or bivalent form. That is, *veldig* does stand out as markedly normative in otherwise dialectal speech now that it is so widely used by self-identified Valdresmål speakers, even occurring unproblematically in self-conscious talk *about* dialect. *Veldig* is not Valdresmål per se, but neither is it perceived as an intrusion from "city-talk" or Bokmål, and contemporary use patterns support the argument that this is the case for many other examples of lexical shift among Valdresmål speakers as well. Still, the overall pattern of decreasing use of words like *grådig* and *grepa* across generations continues to point to the centripetal, unifying force of normative language in the long term.

Dative Case

After "unique" or "unusual" words, dative case grammar comes in as a close second among Valdresmål features that people are highly aware of as being in decline. As in other languages and varieties with a dative case, this is a grammatical system primarily used to mark the indirect object in a sentence or phrase, as well as used with a set of prepositions whose objects either always take the dative case or do so when describing location (rather than direction or movement). Whereas in English the pronouns "he" and "him" distinguish subject (or nominative) case from object case, with "him" used for both direct and indirect objects, in Valdresmål some pronouns can distinguish between direct and indirect objects: *(ha)n* (him) for direct object or accusative case, and *ho(no)* (him) for indirect object or dative case. In addition to pronouns, suffixed definite articles ("the" as a noun ending) and indefinite plural markers (like "-(e)s" in English) also have distinct forms in dative case.

The complete dative case system for Valdresmål was thoroughly documented in the middle of the twentieth century (Aars 1963), but today regular use of dative case forms appears to be on its last legs. In Kvåle's Valdresmål study from the 1990s, only about 5 percent of the teenagers surveyed reported using dative case forms, while their parents used the dative case about 40 percent of the time with prepositions and 22 percent of the time for indirect objects (Kvåle 1999, 134–6). Less than half of the middle-aged and younger people in my recordings use dative case pronouns (like the above example of *ho(no)* "him"). Among younger dative-case users, only a few use dative forms consistently; most vary between using dative and accusative (direct object) forms in grammatical contexts that would have historically required the dative, showing a merged dative-to-accusative pattern. And many older Valdres residents also use dative case forms inconsistently in socially occurring speech. On the other hand, several of the middle-aged and younger dialect speakers I have talked to *do* use the dative case, some of them virtually all the time. These individuals appear to be exceptions to the general rule and told me they made a conscious effort to use dative case. A couple of younger speakers even shared with me that they had sought direct help from middle-aged and older speakers in order to use the dative case correctly and more consistently, showing the power of pro-dialect and purist language ideologies.

Kari, who was around forty at the time, told me about the rapid loss of dative case from one generation to the next in her family, reflecting a feeling of insecurity about dative forms that is common among younger speakers, who are sometimes criticized by older, more competent dative-case users for using dative forms incorrectly.

> *Foreldrudn mine e jo fortsatt støe på dativformadn. Men det e jo ikkji e. Så der e det nok noko som er i ferd med å dø ut med min generasjon og kanskje neste. E kan fortsatt klare noko no så e prøva me innimellom å teste det på mama. Ja vart dette her rettigt, ikkji sant? Mens det e noko som dei har inne. So dei har fått inn med morsmjølke på ein anna måte. Så det e nok i ferd med å bli borte.*
>
> My parents are still surefooted in using dative forms. But I'm not. So it's something that's about to die out with my generation and maybe the next one. I can still manage some [dative case] so once in a while I try to test it out on my mom. Like was that correct, you know? While it's something that they just have down. That they've gotten in with their mothers' milk in a different way. So it's on its way out.

This pattern of rapid dative loss is not uncommon across the remaining dative-case dialects in central Norway, from the regions north of the Oslo area toward Trøndelag, where the city of Trondheim is located. In Gudbrandsdal and Hallingdal, the rural districts on either side of Valdres, dative case has also been in steep decline for at least several decades (Beito 1979; Jenshus 1986; Berge Rudi 2007; Sandøy 2011).

Still, there are a few linguistic forms involving dative prepositions that remain in regular use across generations in Valdres, the most common and salient of which is *å vera på stølé* (to be at the mountain farm), where the noun *ein støl* (a mountain farm) takes the suffixed dative article *–é* (the) rather than the otherwise usual *–en*. The latter is found in the contrasting accusative prepositional construction *å reise på stølen* (to go to the mountain farm), which does not take the dative ending, because it involves directional movement. In Kvåle's survey, as well, *på stølé* was the dative form most frequently used by both teenagers and their parents in Valdres. The contrast between dative *på stølé* and accusative *på stølen* is also a very popular one to cite in lay discussions of the dative case in Valdres, almost certainly because it refers to a highly valued and culturally central place and activity – going to, and being at, the traditional summer mountain farm. The persistence of dative-case *på stølé* may therefore be an example of linguistic calcification, where a feature is preserved in limited contexts and not throughout the system. Despite the resilience of *på stølé*, however, the Valdresmål dative case system is clearly no longer intact, and this is undoubtedly a result of pressure from, and intense exposure to, normative varieties of Norwegian, both spoken and written, none of which has preserved the dative case.

The Vowel System

One of the most understudied areas for Norwegian in general is the vowel system (Kristoffersen 2000, 10). This is understandable, given the sheer amount of lexical and morphological (word-structure) variation across Norwegian dialects and the degree of popular interest in surface-level features. When I ask people in Valdres to describe the dialect or name some of its features, they almost always turn to words first, then things like noun- or verb-suffixes (morphology) and, much more rarely, consonant sounds. No one has ever told me that vowel pronunciation is an important component of Valdresmål. However, when it comes to language change over time in Valdres, there is plenty going on below the surface, and shifts in the vowel system are readily apparent to the trained ear. For the purpose of systematic analysis of change over time, vowels are also especially well suited, because, unlike individual words, they occur frequently in any extended sample of connected speech. Perhaps even more importantly, because vowels are not among the linguistic features that most Valdres speakers are consciously aware of as local or regional markers, they are less likely to vary significantly based on the topic of conversation or the audience. As with many Valdresmål words and grammatical features, Valdresmål vowel patterns have shifted toward normative, urban ones over the last century.

In terms of speech production, we can think of vowel sounds as determined primarily by the position of a speaker's tongue, both vertically and horizontally, which shapes the space in the oral cavity as air flows through and speech sounds are produced. In the vertical plane, we raise the tongue high in the oral cavity to produce a vowel sound like that found in most North American pronunciations of the English word "beet," represented as /i/ in the International Phonetic Alphabet (IPA), while we lower the tongue for the vowel in "bot," written as /a/ in IPA. In the horizontal plane, we also push the tongue forward to make the vowel sound in "beet," and we pull it back for the vowel in "boot," written as /u/ in IPA. (Try these contrasts out for yourself, if you are not already familiar with the idea of vowel articulation!) A third determining factor for vowel sounds is whether the lips are rounded, which they are for English "boot" but not for "beet" or "bot." While English does not have lip-rounding as a sole distinguishing feature for any vowels, Norwegian does, specifically for high front vowels. Finally, also unlike English, Norwegian has long and short vowels, with duration being the primary distinguishing feature; long vowels can be represented by a colon following the vowel symbol. In addition to *monophthongal* or regular, single-sound vowels, Valdresmål also has three *diphthongal* vowels, which combine two vowel sounds: /ai/, /au/, and /ɔi/. These are similar to the diphthongal vowels in US Midwestern pronunciations of the English words "bite," "bout," and "boy."

Linguists are trained to identify vowel front-/back-ness, height, lip rounding, and contrasting vowel length by ear, but we can get an even more precise picture through acoustic analysis of speech recordings. Vowels and other speech sounds are composed of groups of sound waves with multiple layers at different frequencies bundled together to form complex waves. We can easily hear and identify pitch, which linguists call *fundamental frequency* or F0, but there are also other sound waves occurring simultaneously at higher frequencies. When we measure speech-sound waves in Hertz (i.e., wave cycles per second), we find that vowels have additional wave frequencies corresponding roughly to vertical (high-low) and horizontal (front-back) tongue position, and these are referred to as F1 and F2, respectively. Using measurements of F1 and F2 from the middle of each vowel, it is possible to produce a visual representation of the vowel system by plotting F1 on the y-axis and F2 on the x-axis. Complete vowel system plots look more or less like a trapezoid with a wider top and narrower base, as shown in Figures 4.1–4.4. In this case, it is the arrangement of

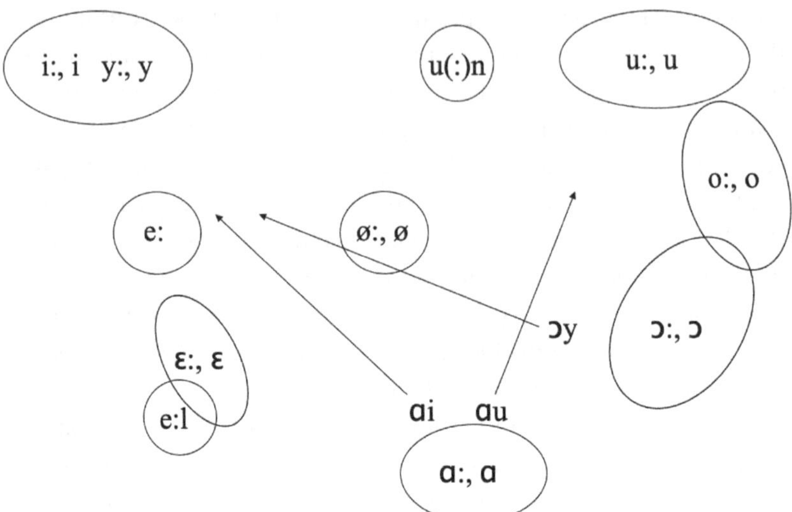

Figure 4.1. Vowel diagram for six Valdresmål speakers born 1920–39, with vowel "height" displayed on the the *y*-axis and "front" vowels to the right and "back" vowels to the left on the *x*-axis.

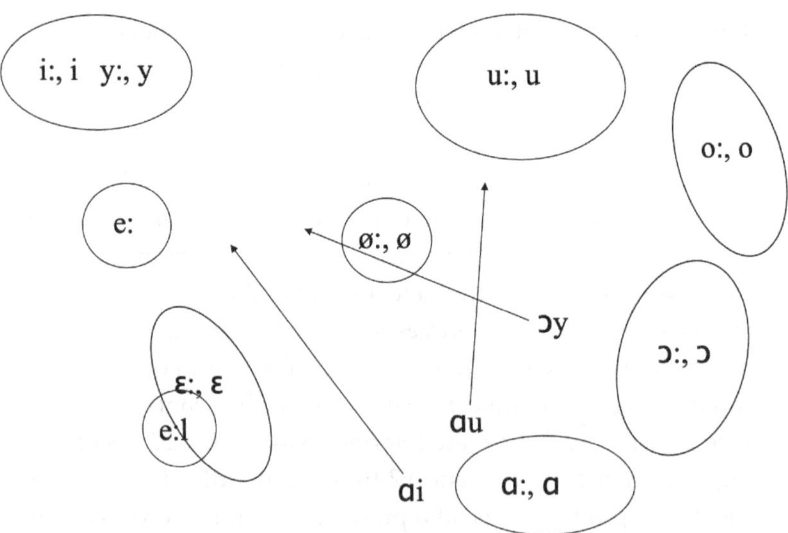

Figure 4.2. Vowel diagram for six Valdresmål speakers born 1940–59, showing /u/ moving forward (to the left), compared to the previous generation.

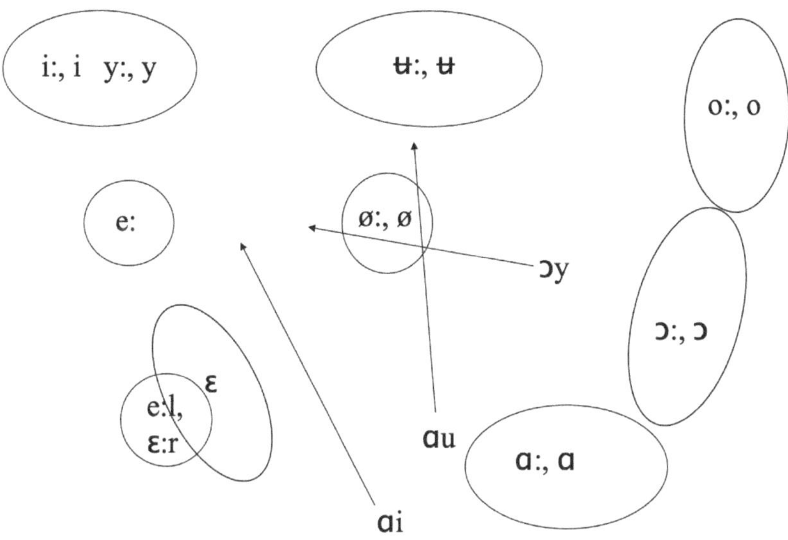

Figure 4.3. Vowel diagram for six Valdresmål speakers born 1960–79, showing fronted /ʉ/ and raised /o/ and /ɔ/, compared to the previous generation.

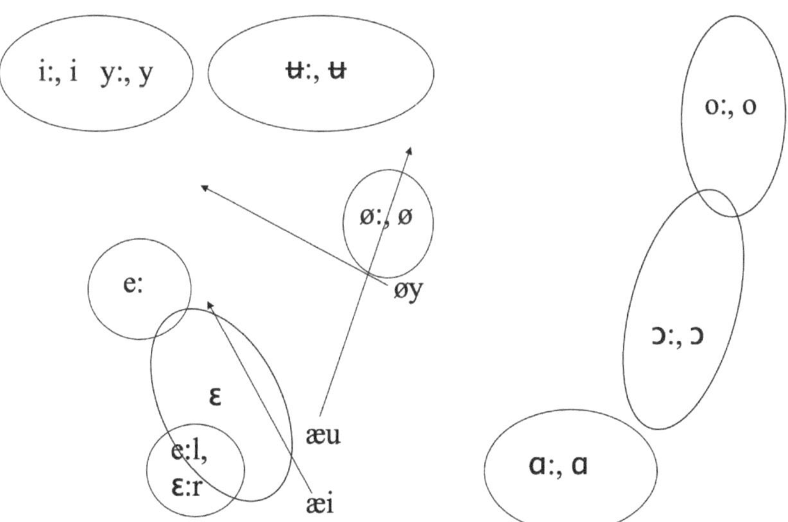

Figure 4.4. Vowel diagram for six Valdresmål speakers born 1980–90, showing more radically fronted /ʉ/, further raised /o/ and /ɔ/, firmly backed /a/, and fronted diphthongs (represented by arrows), compared to the previous generation.

vowels within the plot and how their relative positions are different across age groups that is of primary interest.

To analyze changes in vowel pronunciation over time for Valdresmål, I measured, plotted, and compared the complete vowel systems of twenty-four self-identified Valdres dialect speakers using casual interview recordings of around an hour each. I included a representative sample of three men and three women, all cisgender, from each of four generational groups, born 1920–39, 1940–59, 1960–79, and 1980–90. Everyone in the oldest generation was retired, and two people in the 1940–59 generation were newly semi-retired. In the youngest generation, half were still in high school or college and had part-time jobs. Everyone else had full-time jobs. Speakers' current and former occupational fields included agriculture, architecture, education, engineering, health care, human resources, journalism, machine operation, marketing, military, performance art, public administration, social work, retail sales, sports, and vehicle repair, with many having worked in multiple fields. All had completed either academic or trade-based secondary school, except a few who were then in their final year, and about half had some postsecondary education, ranging up to the equivalent of a master's degree. So this was a diverse group, representative of the many, varied life experiences people have in contemporary Valdres.

To measure each speaker's vowels, I used Praat acoustic analysis software (Boersma and Weenink 2008). For each of twenty-one Norwegian vowels, including the three diphthongs, I found up to five occurrences (fewer for rarer vowels) in three specific linguistic environments (see Labov et al. 1972). I then measured F1 and F2 near the middle of the vowel for monophthongs and at two points, about one-fourth and three-fourths of the way through, for diphthongs. This amounted to a total of 180–200 vowel *tokens*, or individual occurrences, per speaker and nearly 4,500 tokens across the twenty-four-speaker sample. To compare speakers' vowel systems, I used an online vowel plotting program called NORM (Thomas and Kendall 2007) to create visual representations. (All of the individual speaker plots are available as an appendix in Strand 2009.)

Comparing vowel plots within and across generations, there is general consistency within each age group but clear and consistent differences across them, showing significant change in apparent time.

The vowel systems for each generational group are summarized in Figures 4.1, 4.2, 4.3, and 4.4. These diagrams are meant to provide an easily readable approximation of the main patterns for each age group. They do not represent exact F1 and F2 means; instead, they show general, patterned differences, accounting for both inter- and intra-speaker variation.

The relative position of vowels for the oldest generation (born 1920–39), shown in Figure 4.1, corresponds to the traditional Valdres vowel pattern described in Kvåle (1999). The long /u:/ vowel, as in *bud* ("bid" or "messenger"; sounds like Midwestern US English "boot"), is far back (to the right on the vowel chart) at the top the vowel space, except when followed by a nasal consonant (like /n/ or /m/) for several speakers, which "pulls" it forward toward the front (to the left). For this oldest group of speakers, the initial sounds in the diphthongs are also toward the back, so, for example, a word like *dau* (dead) starts with a low, mid-back vowel and rises to a high, back vowel sound (similar to "bout" in Northern US English). Excluding pre-nasal tokens for /u/, all of the back vowels line up nearly vertically, with F2 ≤ 1000 Hz or so, which is quite far "back" in acoustic terms.

There is one outlier for this traditional back-vowel pattern in the oldest speaker group, who, unlike the other five speakers, had lived and attended postsecondary school in Oslo for several years in the 1950s before returning to Valdres, which is a likely explanation. In the 1950s and still today, the typical Oslo vowel system had a different pattern, with the /u/ vowel pronounced farther forward, so much so that it is not a back vowel at all but a high, mid vowel sound, written as /ʉ/ in IPA. American English has a similar pattern in regional vowel pronunciation on the West Coast, where words like "boot" and "dude" are often pronounced with a high, mid-to-front vowel, sometimes far enough forward that they sound like "bit" or "did" among Midwestern speakers.

The fronted-/u/ pattern in Oslo speech is just one difference from the Valdres vowel system found among the oldest group of speakers. In addition, the remaining back vowels are raised in the normative Oslo vowel pattern: the vowel in Norwegian words like *bot* (monetary fine) is pronounced as /u:/, and in Norwegian words like *båt* (boat), the vowel is pronounced as /o:/. Contrastingly, as shown in Figure 4.1, elderly speakers from Valdres use mid-back /o:/ in *bot* and low-back /ɔ:/ in *båt* (the latter of which is similar to US Midwestern English "bought").

Among the next-oldest generation of Valdresmål speakers (born 1940–59), there is more consistent, though still relatively slight, /u/-fronting (shifted to the left on the vowel chart), as well as some /o/-raising, as shown in Figure 4.2. This points to the beginnings of a vowel system change called a *chain shift,* in which an initial change in the pronunciation of one vowel has the effect of "pulling" or "pushing" others around in the vowel space (Labov 1994). In this case, once Valdres speakers start using fronted /u/ sounds, the other back vowels are pulled along counterclockwise, effectively moving them upward, with /o/ starting to move toward where /u/ used to be. And the chain only grows and strengthens from there.

Among the generation born 1960–79, whose vowel patterns are shown in Figure 4.3, /u/ is moderately fronted to /ʉ/, located roughly halfway between the high-front vowels and the back vowel /o/, which has begun rising into the high-back /u/ space. We also see the next link in the chain shift among this generation, with /ɔ/ rising up toward where /o/ was for the oldest speakers.

Finally, for the youngest speakers (born 1980–90), Figure 4.4 shows that /u/ is now more radically fronted to /ʉ/, while the back vowels remain about the same as for the preceding generation. In addition to the back-vowel chain shift, the nucleus (starting point) of each of the diphthongs also appears to have moved forward over time, with the youngest Valdres speakers having very fronted diphthongs. This pattern is also aligned with well-established Oslo speech norms.

In the vowel system, then, both the back-vowel chain shift and diphthong-fronting are further examples of long-term convergence toward normative urban speech. These apparent-time vowel changes across generations are very clear and consistent, even among speakers who make the most use of distinctive Valdresmål words and grammar. Because vowels are not considered "dialect" in the same way as those surface-level features, their changes are not problematized in the same way as lexical or dative-case loss. As a result, vowels are not a focus for those hoping to maintain "traditional" Valdresmål, and this example of linguistic convergence toward normative patterns seems to have proceeded quite consistently and without much concern.

PRO-DIALECT IDEOLOGIES, RESILIENCE, AND INNOVATION

The above examples show long-term dialect shift toward regional urban norms in lexicon, morphology, and phonology. However, there are also many Valdresmål features that do *not* appear to be undergoing this sort of normalizing change and can be described as examples of linguistic nonconvergence or possibly even divergence or innovation among younger speakers. In Bakhtin's (1981) terms, this kind of multidirectional change speaks to the "centrifugal" forces and the heteroglossic nature of language in society, as discussed in Chapter 2. In contrast to the homogenizing, centripetal linguistic forces embodied in dialect leveling and normalization, the centrifugal forces manifested in language variation of all sorts hinder and sometimes work against sociolinguistic processes of standardization and homogenization. Importantly, as Bakhtin (1981) wrote, "at any given moment of its evolution, language is stratified not only into linguistic dialects in the strict sense of the word … but also – and for us this is the essential point – into languages that are socio-ideological" (272). Language variation and nonstandard varieties, which reflect broader social variation and stratification, represent a constant barrier to complete homogenization, and shifts in the dynamics of language change may therefore reflect changes in social relations and language ideologies.

In the case of contemporary Valdresmål, certain "traditional" features have become more resilient as the dialect has been revalued in the twenty-first century, and many younger speakers appear eager to avoid using forms that are markedly normative or urban-sounding in the local context. Adults in Valdres today are often well aware of these changes, having witnessed the shift from pro-urban to pro-local language ideologies during their lifetimes. Audunn, a local theater producer who also worked with high school drama students, told me that, in contrast to when she was a teenager in the early 1990s, "it's almost more permissible *now* to speak Valdresmål than it was then. There's something about the authenticity [*rotekte*] and the Norwegianness … It's more with the times now than it was then."

Audunn's observations were supported by other younger dialect speakers' reflections, as well. Sigrunn, a college student and talented skier, recounted to me that, while her own dialect use and attitudes had not changed over time, her sister's and many classmates' had, especially during middle and high school in the late 1990s.

> *Systa mi, ho bynte å knote litt meire då slek når @ ho @ gikk på ungdomsskule @@ så der vart det – då vart det kanskje litt meire @ tema då. Det synst mø vart veldi feil. At det passa kji. @@ … Men nå prata ho dialekt att. @@ Så det va – ho va litt meir urban i den perioda der.*
>
> My sister, she started to *knot* [i.e., use urban and Bokmål forms] a little more when @ she @ went to middle school @@ so then it became – then it became a little more @ of an issue. We thought that that was really wrong. That it didn't fit. @@ But now she speaks more dialect again. @@ So it was – she was a little more urban in that phase.

I asked Sigrunn whether she thought anything had changed since she was in middle school, and her answer demonstrated clear and thoughtful awareness of shifts in the sociolinguistic climate.

> *Når e gikk på ungdomsskule og på viaregående va det nok mange som bynte å knote, meire tå dei som egentle prata dialekt altså. Det va det. For det va nok – då fekk n jo meire påvirkning frå andre. Fekk nye venne og vart kjent me følk frå Fagernes for eksempel, der dei ikkji prata så mykjy dialekt. […] Og fekk meir påvirkning derifrå. Og kanskje va det kanskje ikkji så status å prate dialekt eh den tie der. Men nå – dei siste åre tru e det e – har e inntrykk tå at det e mindre knoting egentle slek når dei kjem på ungsomskule og viaregående. At det e litt meire status å halde på dialekte. At fleire gjere det. Så det syns e e veldi positivt.*
>
> When I was in middle school and in high school there were a lot of people who started to *knot* [i.e., use urban and Bokmål forms], more people who actually spoke dialect I mean. There were. Because it was – you got more influenced by others. Got new friends and met people from Fagernes for example, where they don't speak as much dialect. […] And got more pressure from there. And maybe it was maybe not so [high] status to speak dialect at the time. But now – the last few years I think it's – I have

> the impression that there's less *knoting* actually when they get to middle school and high school. That it's a little higher status to stick with your dialect. That more people do that. So I think that's really positive.

Halvard, another 1990s teen, even told me about a group of friends who made fairly dramatic turns *toward* broad (more strongly marked) Valdresmål during high school, as well as toward more local forms of youth culture. Despite having "grown up quite snobby down in Fagernes," Halvard told me, as high schoolers some of his friends "suddenly switched over to really broad Vallers." According to Halvard, some of them also took up things like chewing tobacco and an interest in cars and country music, which were decidedly rural practices that he contrasted with hashish and punk in the regional urban youth scene of that era.

Taking these local insights into account, in addition to what we already know about the presently high status of rural dialects in central Norway, it is clear there have been recent, significant changes in language ideologies and linguistic practice among youth in Valdres. The following sections describe, as above, a small but representative group of linguistic features, this time showing evidence of resilience, re-emergence, and innovation for marked dialect forms among younger speakers.

Lexical Resilience

While there is strong evidence of long-term lexical shift toward urban norms, there are also a fair number of distinctive words in contemporary Valdresmål that are used nearly categorically across age groups. These include personal pronouns, question words, prepositions, and other common "function" words, all of which occur much more frequently than most "content" words. On the whole, these are among the most resilient marked forms in Valdresmål today, and they represent a significant degree of nonconvergence with regional urban norms.

Personal pronouns may well be the most consciously oriented-to dialect features in Valdresmål. In particular, the first-person singular *e* (I) and first-person plural *mø* (we) are highly salient forms and

Table 4.1. Common Valdresmål personal pronouns, in comparison to Bokmål and Nynorsk forms

Valdresmål	Bokmål	Nynorsk	English gloss
e	*jeg*	*eg*	I
mø	*vi*	*vi/me*	we
ho	*hun*	*ho*	she
dei	*de*	*dei*	they
dikkan	*dere*	*dykk*	you-pl., object

contrast markedly with regionally normative *jeg* and *vi*, respectively (see Table 4.1). In Kvåle's survey (1999), *e* (I) was the most widely used Valdresmål form, with 100 percent of adults and 86 percent of teenagers saying they used *e* for first-person singular. The plural *mø* (we) was also used by 98 percent of adults and about three-quarters of middle- and high schoolers. In my own data from the last decade and a half, all of the self-identified Valdresmål speakers I have recorded use first-person singular *e* (I) categorically (i.e., 100 percent of the time), including in interviews, conversational speech, and media appearances. Nearly all of them also use first-person plural *mø* (we) categorically, with a few notable exceptions: three who use *vi* only rarely and lived outside Valdres for a time prior to 1980, and a fourth born and raised in Fagernes in the 1950s–60s, who used *vi* consistently, which is not unusual in the semi-urban commercial center and former station town.

More significantly, none of the younger dialect speakers I recorded (born 1960–90) used normative first-person pronouns, although two told me they had used both *jeg* and *vi* when living in Oslo for extended periods and still occasionally used them when hanging out with Oslo friends. For others, however, first-person *e* and *mø* are too strong an element of their linguistic identity to part with, even though they may have normalized other dialect features in situations outside of Valdres. John, who was born in the 1960s, told me about modifying his dialectal speech to avoid comments from peers and professors at college in Oslo in the 1980s. But, he said, "I remember just with *mø*. I could never say *vi* there. It was always *mø*." Retention of local first-person pronouns is common in surrounding regions, too, with marked singular forms used by upwards of 90 percent of residents in the nearby districts of Hallingdal and Gudbrandsdal (Berge Rudi 2007), Røros (Røyneland 2005), and Sogndal (Stokstad 2007). And first-person plural forms have been even more resilient in Valdres than in many other places, including neighboring Hallingdal, where plural *me* (we) is used only about half the time, increasingly displaced by *vi* (Thoengen 1994; Berge Rudi 2007).

In Valdres, according to Kvåle's (1999) survey and my own data, several other non-normative personal pronouns have also been fairly resistant to pressure from normative forms, including third-person singular feminine *ho* (she), third-person plural *dei* (they), and second-person plural object *dikkan* (you-pl.). In Bokmål these are *hun* (she), *de* (they), and *dere* (you-pl.), while in Nynorsk they may be written *ho*, *dei*, and *dykk*, in closer alignment with spoken Valdresmål.

Not far behind personal pronouns in their persistence are Valdresmål's marked question words. According to Kvåle's survey (1999), virtually all parents and roughly 80 percent of middle- and high school students reported using Valdresmål question words in the 1990s, which begin with /k/ sounds in contrast to regionally normative /v/- forms. Linguistically, these differences are more phonetic (about sounds) than lexical, but they are talked about as different words in popular discourse. In my recordings, I find nearly categorical use of the question words *ko* (what), *kem* (who[m]), *ko(r)* (where), and *kofør* (why), which contrast with the Bokmål and normative Eastern spoken forms *hva, hvem, hvor,* and *hvorfor*, as shown in Table 4.2. Like Valdresmål, most Nynorsk question words begin with *k*, but *kva, kven, kvar,* and *kvifor* are not much closer otherwise.

There are also quite a few "content" words tied to local traditions of small-scale dairy production that are still in regular use, with no evidence of displacement by normative forms. These include the words *kyr* (cow), *støl* (summer mountain farm), and *mjølk* (milk), which contrast with *ku, seter,* and *melk* in Bokmål and urban Eastern speech; both *kyr* and *mjølk* are represented in Nynorsk, the latter briefly discussed in Chapter 2. In the rural setting of Valdres, all of these are culturally central and thus occur frequently, making them more likely candidates for retention than lower-frequency words or those tied more closely to nonlocal activities.

Table 4.2. Common Valdresmål question words, in comparison to Bokmål and Nynorsk forms

Valdresmål	Bokmål	Nynorsk	English gloss
ko	*hva*	*kva*	what
kem	*hvem*	*kven*	who
ko(r)	*hvor*	*kvar*	where
koför	*hvorfor*	*kvifor*	why

Continuity and Innovation in Morphology

Moving beyond words, among the linguistic features of Valdresmål that lay speakers are most conscious of are its distinctive definite plural noun suffixes *–adn, –idn,* and *–udn,* which are all forms of plural "the," positioned at the end of the word in Norwegian rather than before it like in English. These pluralizing morphemes often came up in metalinguistic interviews, where I was told repeatedly that *–adn, –idn,* and *–udn* were among the most characteristic elements of the Valdres dialect. Rather amusingly, the definite plural suffixes are almost always described meta-morphologically as *endingadn* (the endings), often with a wry smile or a chuckle, as people are aware of the necessity of using *–adn* in order to talk about *–adn, –idn,* and *–udn* as a group.

While Valdresmål has *–adn, –idn,* and *–udn* as definite plural suffixes for masculine and feminine nouns across cases, the standard definite plural suffix in Bokmål is *–ene,* while Nynorsk uses *–ene* for feminine and *–ane* for masculine nouns in the definite plural form. The Valdresmål suffixes *–adn, –idn,* and *–udn* are distinct enough from regionally normative *–ene* in Bokmål and urban Eastern speech to attract a lot of metalinguistic commentary from nonlocals. According to many people in Valdres, these unusual endings are an especially salient feature that outsiders readily notice and attempt to imitate, though often unsuccessfully.

In her survey of dialect use among Valdres teenagers, Kvåle (1999) found that these distinctive definite plural noun suffixes were used more than many other marked morphological features. Kvåle's results indicate that regionally normative *–ene* suffixes were used by about 18 percent of middle- and high school students, while none of the adult dialect speakers reported using *–ene.* In my own recordings, normative *–ene* suffixes for definite plural nouns are similarly rare, with only isolated occurrences across age groups. The dialect of Hallingdal, Valdres's neighbor to the southwest, also uses *–adn*, *–idn*, and *–udn*, though the more regionally widespread forms *–an*, *–in*, and *–un* have become increasingly common there (Venås 1977; Thoengen 1994; Berge Rudi 2007). In Sogndal, to the northwest of Valdres, *–adn* and *–edn* also remain in use among youth (Haugen 2004, 221), and, to the northeast in Gudbrandsdal, the traditional forms *–an*, *–in*, and *–un*, have held strong, too (Berge Rudi 2007, 92). On the other side of Gudbrandsdal, Røyneland (2005) concluded that, in the early 2000s, it was "absolutely certain that the standard form *–ene* has in no way gained acceptance either in Røros or Tynset" (359). Like personal pronouns and question words for lexicon, definite plural noun suffixes are among the highest-frequency morphological features; they are heard and used all the time, and they are salient dialect features for locals and nonlocals alike.

There are important points of nonconvergence in Valdresmål verb morphology, as well. Among the most interesting and potentially innovative are the infinitive and present-tense markers for the irregular verb meaning "to do." Historically, the infinitive form *å gjera* (to do) was used consistently, but today Valdresmål speakers use both *å gjera* and *å gjere* as infinitive forms, with younger speakers using the *–e* ending more often. In Kvåle's survey, 100 percent of adult respondents indicated that they use *–a* for the class of verbs that *å gjera* belongs to, while 67 percent of teenagers reported using *–a*. This is a more linguistically complicated example than many of those discussed above, in that a shift from *å gjera* to *å gjere* may involve both convergence and nonconvergence at the same time. In urban Eastern speech and in Bokmål, *å gjøre* is the normative infinitive for "to do." Shifting to the normative *–e* infinitive marker looks like convergence in verb morphology, while the unrounded vowel /e/ is still retained in the root and contrasts markedly with normative /ø/.

Among the dialect speakers with whom I recorded interviews, *å gjera* is used the vast majority of the time across age groups, accounting for over 85 percent of all tokens. But younger people tend to alternate between *å gjera* and *å gjere* more than older folks, and they also make occasional use of normative *å gjøre*, a form that some older speakers find to be an irritating example of dialect shift. Marie, a life-long rural Valdres resident in her seventies at the time, had a litany of complaints against young Valdresmål speakers, and their use of normative *å gjøre* was something that especially irked her.

(1) M: *No byna ho å vaskast ut.*
Now [the dialect] is starting to get washed out.
(2) T: *Ja?*
Yeah?
(3) M: *Ja, ho* ***gjera*** *det.*
Yes, it is.
(4) T: *E det noko spesielt du ha merka forandra seg?*
Is there anything in particular you've noticed is changing?
(5) M: *Nei. E veit kji. . Dei. . .*
No. I don't know. . They. . .
(6) *Dei – ungadn no ska* ***gjøra*** *det, sei dei.*
They – kids today are going to **do** that, they say.
(7) *E seie ja, mø ska* ***gjera*** *det.*
I say yes, we'll **do** that.
(8) T: @
(9) M: *Nei, men liksom sleke enkle ord. Som dei vrir lite på.*
No, but like these simple words. That they twist a little bit.
(10) *Det e kji nødvendigt det.*
It's just not necessary.

Marie is right that younger speakers use normative *å gjøre* more often than people her age, but my data also clearly show that the marked local form *å gjera* remains in use at high rates across age groups.

In addition to variation in the infinitive, the traditional Valdresmål present-tense form *gjera* (do/does) is used quite consistently among middle-aged and older speakers. However, present-tense *gjera* also seems to be competing with two new "compromise" forms, *gjere* and *gjer*, and also with the normative present-tense form *gjør* (do/does), which is found in regional urban speech and in Bokmål. Written Nynorsk, however, uses *gjer* in the present tense.

Historically, the alternating use of *gjera* and *gjere* in the present tense differentiated between singular and plural subjects, with *–a* for singular and *–e* for plural, but this does not explain contemporary variation in the present tense. By the 1950s, singular-plural present-tense

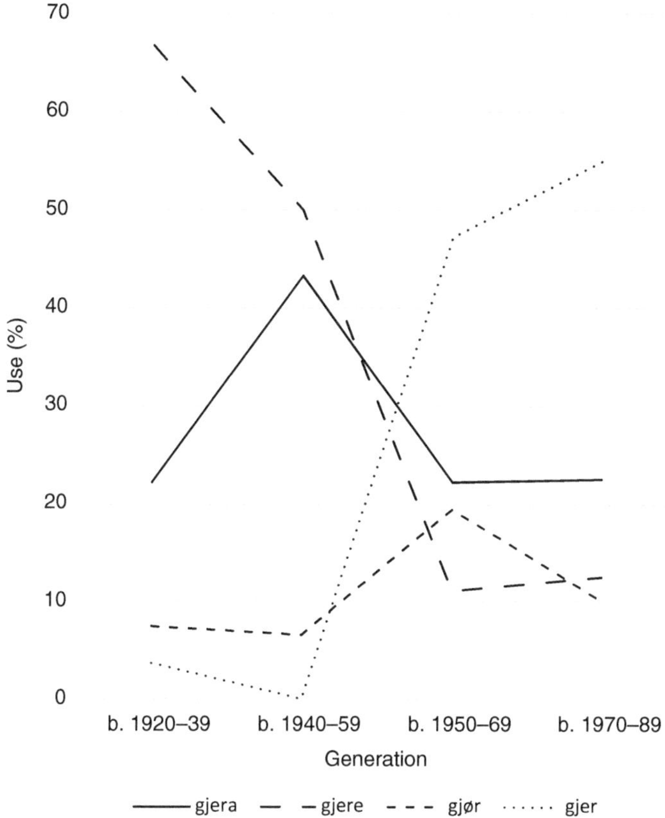

Figure 4.5. Variation in present-tense "do" realization by generation, $N = 222$.

marking was already regarded as archaic (Beito 1959), and Kvåle declared it "as good as dead" by the 1990s (1999, 96). Curious to see whether it could possibly have re-emerged, I included singular or plural subject as a variable when coding my data for present-tense "do" and ran it through GoldVarb X, a multivariate statistical analysis program (Sankoff et al. 2005). This confirmed there was no correlation between subject number and present-tense suffix, even among the oldest speakers, though it is possible that the historical existence of both forms has contributed to their contemporary coexistence.

As Figure 4.5 shows, regionally normative present-tense *gjør* (do) occurs among all generations of Valdresmål speakers, indicating long-term pressure from urban Eastern speech norms and written Bokmål. More interesting, however, is that a new present-tense form in spoken Valdresmål, *gjer*, is widespread among speakers born after 1960, and it is used more than twice as frequently as normative *gjør* in my recordings. In fact, normative *gjør* is more frequent among those born in the 1960s and 1970s than it is among the youngest generation, those born between 1980 and 1990. This suggests a recent turn away from regional urban norms, and it may be an example of an expanding, innovative dialect form in contemporary Valdresmål. Likely drawing from written Nynorsk as something that is definitively "not Bokmål," uptake of the minority written form *gjer* in local speech may be motivated by pro-dialect, pro-local ideologies. Clearly, local variation for this high-frequency verb is complex, as it is affected by the centripetal forces of Bokmål, Nynorsk, and urban speech norms in several distinct ways. Analyzing this complex variation in ethnographic and historical context, I believe the expansion of *gjer* as a new spoken form in Valdresmål demonstrates the power of counteracting, centrifugal sociolinguistic forces, resisting and diverging from dominant regional and national norms.

New Life for an Old Diphthong

A final example of innovation brings us back to vowel phonology and the diphthong /øy/. This combination-vowel sound is used by Valdresmål speakers in ordinary, expected ways in most linguistic environments. But in Valdresmål /øy/ also occurs as a variant of monophthongal /ø/ in certain pre-rhotic environments, when /ø/ comes just before an /r/ sound. In words like *øyra* (ear) and *å høyre* (to hear), Valdresmål has diphthongal /øyr/, a pattern retained from Old Norse that is consistently monophthongized to /ør/ in normative Eastern speech and Bokmål, which have *ør* (ear) and *å høre* (to hear). This is a relatively rare phonetic feature, but diphthongal /øyr/ is an especially interesting vowel sound in contemporary Valdresmål, as its use seems to be expanding among younger generations of dialect speakers. Like the examples of dialect resilience and innovation in lexicon and morphology above, /øyr/ expansion is likely motivated by pro-dialect, anti-normalization ideologies, pushing back against the pressures of urban speech patterns and the dominant written norm of Bokmål.

Although it is a low-frequency sound pattern overall, a striking example of the expanding use of /øyr/ is found across tenses of the common verb *å høyre* (to hear/listen) and the prepositional construction *å høyre te* (to belong to). For this verb, there is widespread, cross-generational use of diphthongal /øyr/ (realized as /ɔyr/ by older speakers) in the infinitive *å høyre* (to hear), in present tense *høyra* (hear[s]), and in passive voice *høyres(t)* or *høyrast* (sounds), among Valdres dialect speakers. In all of these tenses, /øyr/ precedes another vowel, making /r/ intervocalic, and the diphthongal variant is used about 60–75 percent of the time across age groups.

At the same time, older speakers in my recordings always use monophthongal /ør/ in past tense *hørde* (heard) and present perfect *ha hørt* (have heard), where /ør/ occurs before alveolar consonants, which are sounds made with the tongue on the alveolar ridge, between the top teeth and hard palate. So, for example, Marie, who was in her seventies, said to me at one point in our interview:

> *Nei det* ***høyre*** *e. E ha* ***hørt*** *det på syskjenbødna mine.*
>
> "No I **hear** it. I've **heard** it among my cousins."

However, many younger-adult Valdresmål speakers use the diphthong in both environments, saying *høyre* in the present tense and *høyrde* in the past tense. Thus, there is not much generational variation in rates of diphthongal versus monophthongal pronunciations in the infinitive, present, or passive tenses. But younger speakers sometimes use diphthongal /øyr/ in the past tense, while older speakers never do in my interview recordings, as shown in Table 4.3.

With relatively few tokens of past tense *hø(y)rde* (heard), it is impossible to draw firm conclusions. However, given that speakers born prior to 1960 *never* use the regionally non-normative diphthongal /øyr/ in past-tense *hørde*, it is remarkable that younger speakers do. And while I did not happen to have any instances of it in the interview data I used for the statistics reported in Table 4.3, in casual

Table 4.3. Use of monophthongal and diphthongal *høyre* (hear), including variant, number of occurrences, and percent of occurrences in four tenses, across four generations of speakers

Generation	Infinitive *høre* *høyre*			Past *hørde* *høyrde*			Present perfect *ha hørt* *ha høyrt*			Passive *høres(t)* *høyres(t)*		
b. 1920–39	ø	17	40%	ø	8	100%	ø	11	100%	ø	1	33%
	øy	26	60%	øy	0	0%	øy	0	0%	øy	2	67%
b. 1940–59	ø	13	27%	ø	14	100%	ø	14	100%	ø	1	50%
	øy	35	73%	øy	0	0%	øy	0	0%	øy	1	50%
b. 1960–79	ø	16	27%	ø	10	71%	ø	11	100%	ø	0	0%
	øy	44	73%	øy	4	29%	øy	0	0%	øy	3	100%
b. 1980–89	ø	11	33%	ø	1	25%	ø	14	100%	ø	2	50%
	øy	22	67%	øy	3	75%	øy	0	0%	øy	2	50%

conversation I have also heard younger speakers using diphthongal /øyr/ in the present perfect *ha høyrt* (have heard), and often across tenses for the common verb *kjøyre* (drive), including past-tense *kjøyrde* (drove). I also hear younger speakers using word-final /øyr/, as in *døyr* (die[s]) and *røyr* (pipe), while older speakers virtually always use monophthongal *dør* and *rør*, as found in Bokmål and normative Eastern speech.

If these diphthongal variants are not a part of the Valdres dialect among older speakers, then where did they come from, and, perhaps more importantly, why are younger dialect speakers using them today? I believe there are both linguistic and ideological factors contributing to generational differences in /øyr/ patterning. Historically, diphthongal /øyr/ occurred only with a tapped or trilled /r/, which was the only /r/ sound in Old Norse and Middle Norwegian. Over the last several centuries, however, a new /r/ sound, called retroflex /r/ (IPA /ɹ/), like the /r/ sound in North American English, became increasingly widespread in Eastern Norway when it occurred before the alveolar consonants /t/, /d/, and /n/. So /r/ is still tapped or trilled most of the time, but most people use a retroflex /r/ (like American English) in /rd/, /rt/, and /rn/ (Kristoffersen 2000). In central Valdres, incorporation of retroflex /r/ in these linguistic environments was probably only complete in the early twentieth century, as some older speakers in Vang parish, the farthest north in Valdres, still do not use retroflex /r/, which is a locally well-known point of linguistic difference. Nynorsk creator Ivar Aasen's wordlists from Valdres and Hallingdal, collected from 1845 to 1866, also contain pre-alveolar /øyr/ words with *høyre* as a root, including, for example, *faahøyrd* (seldom; Aasen 2002). In central Valdres, however, historic /øyr/ was likely monophthongized to /ør/ in pre-alveolar environments not long after that, with retroflex /r/ taking over before /t/, /d/, and /n/. The diphthong was retained elsewhere, yielding the *høyra-hørde* (hear-heard) contrast found among older speakers today.

However, /øyr/ has now resurfaced among younger speakers in pre-alveolar environments, and some of them seem to use it categorically. For instance, in an interview with a forty-something local-food enthusiast from central Valdres, the topic turned to cured ham, a Valdres specialty similar to Italian prosciutto or Spanish serrano ham, and the relatively little-used word for "tenderize" came up, drawing my attention to an unusual-to-me use of /øyr/.

(1) H: *[E] driv å salta skinko sjøl*
[I] salt-cure hams myself
(2) *o så ha mø – ha e bynt då med noen år sida*
and we've – I started a few years ago
(3) *at mø høppa på skinka. <pause> Før å – <pause>*
that we hop on the ham. <pause> To – <pause>
(4) T: *Ja.* ***Mørna.***
Yeah. Tenderize.
(5) H: ***Møyrna*** *ho liksom.*
Like tenderize it.

I recognized that Harald was searching for the word for "tenderize" in line 3, so I proffered *mørna* in line 4, having only ever heard and seen it with a monophthongal /ø/. But Harald repeated it back to me, a split-second later, as *møyrna*, with a strong diphthong, in line 5. The phonetic contrast was strikingly clear in this example and further evidence of the re-emergence of pre-alveolar /øyr/ in Valdresmål.

If younger dialect speakers have not acquired pre-alveolar /øyr/ organically via an unbroken chain of Valdresmål speakers, then it may be that the Nynorsk written norm is a source of support, as it seems to be for present-tense *gjer* (do), discussed above. The possibility of mutual influence between written and spoken language has been demonstrated in a variety of places, including in second dialect acquisition in English in the UK (Chambers 1988), in the effects of literacy instruction in the new written norm for Catalan in Spain (Carrera-Sabaté 2006), and in Scandinavia, where Pedersen (2005) has concluded that written norms in both Denmark and Sweden have influenced normative spoken language in those countries. As discussed in Chapter 2, it is also evident that written Danish historically exerted influence on spoken language in Oslo, where Danish administration of Norway was once sited.

Looking at possible connections between writing and pronunciation in the Valdresmål case, it is almost certainly significant that all of the speakers using pre-alveolar /øyr/ in my recordings also used Nynorsk as their primary written norm. Nynorsk has forms like *høyrde* and *møyrna*, while Bokmål does not. We might consider this to be an example of *hypercorrection* (Labov 1972), in which speakers are consciously trying to hit an imagined target of linguistic correctness but slightly overshooting by using a known rule in contexts where it does not apply. For pre-alveolar /øyr/, speakers seem to be aiming for "proper" or "traditional" Valdresmål and consciously avoiding normative Eastern speech forms but overgeneralizing the diphthongal variant of /ør/ to contexts beyond those where it is used by older dialect speakers today. Baugh (1992) found a similar kind of "hypocorrection" (as he called it) toward vernacular African American English (AAE) among non-native AAE speakers who were trying to express solidarity with African American communities (1992). But while most examples of hypercorrection and hypocorrection are understood to be grammatically inaccurate, in the case of younger Valdresmål speakers' expanding use of /øyr/, that does not seem to be the case. They *are* overshooting the contemporary dialect pattern among older speakers, but, in "correcting" away from urban speech and Bokmål, they are actually reproducing an even older pattern, as well as using a "spelling pronunciation" aligned with Nynorsk and, in both ways, hitting the ideological target of traditional, rural Norwegian speech, which Nynorsk is often believed to represent.

The linguistic and symbolic-ideological connections to written Nynorsk help explain the phonological trend of re-expanding /øyr/, as well as many other persistent, non-normative lexical and morphological features in contemporary Valdresmål, which often correspond to forms represented in Nynorsk. However, the overall dynamics of dialect change are complicated and multidirectional, showing evidence of many interacting centripetal and centrifugal linguistic forces, some written, some spoken, and variously local, regional, and national.

LINGUISTIC AWARENESS, IDEOLOGY, AND CHANGE

The examples of language change in this chapter show that contemporary Valdresmål is not moving exclusively in the direction of Bokmål and urban regional speech, despite many people's long-term fear that that is inevitable. There are many points of convergence toward dominant norms, to be sure, but there are also many marked dialect features that have remained relatively stable and others that appear to be either new or re-emergent.

Some Valdresmål features are frequently talked about, circulating widely in metalinguistic discourse, so much so that popular awareness of distinctive personal pronouns, like *e* and *mø*, and the definite plural noun endings *–adn, –idn,* and *–udn* has made them virtually defining of Valdresmål. But this is not, and cannot practically be, the case for every dialect feature. Significantly, many of the most resilient marked forms in contemporary Valdresmål, as well as some innovative and expanding features, are represented in written Nynorsk. Of course, not all dialect speakers in Valdres have a strong commitment to Nynorsk, and, as discussed in Chapter 2, some definitely prefer Bokmål for reading and formal writing. But most nevertheless acquired Nynorsk as their first primary written language in Valdres's rural elementary schools.

When we have a situation in which distinctive, traditional forms are being maintained, new ones are gaining ground, and long-term pressure from nearby urban norms continues to be felt, all at the same time, we can see the complicated effects of so much national heteroglossia, both official, in the dual written norm situation, and unofficial, in the persistence of highly distinctive spoken dialects. In contemporary multidirectional change in Valdresmål, we can also observe, up close, many strong, ideologically differentiated linguistic forces interacting at a particular time-point in a relatively small social and geographic space. Bokmål, Nynorsk, urban Eastern speech, and

Valdresmål all pull and push on each other, and the strength of their centripetal or centrifugal forces depends on both the immediate interactional context and the larger sociohistorical moment.

As I hope to have shown in this and earlier chapters, the present sociolinguistic picture is tied to twenty-first-century cultural changes, both local and national, that have reoriented popular and youth culture away from exclusively urban areas, permitting local, and especially rural, forms to re-emerge as valuable and even trendy. A consequence of this revalorization is that many younger Valdres residents have become enthusiastically interested in speaking dialect, and they now claim local, rural identities through dialect use that is in conscious contrast to "snobby," urban ways of speaking and being. Interestingly, while young Valdresmål speakers generally feel much more strongly about maintaining spoken dialect diversity than they do about preserving Nynorsk, the latter still seems to be a force that can support dialect maintenance and also be drawn from to emphasize or reinforce distance from dominant Bokmål and regional speech norms.

While it is difficult, if not impossible, to definitively "prove" the ideological motivation of any particular linguistic change, taking an ethnographic approach that seriously considers local viewpoints suggests, in this case, that observable changes in Valdresmål are not random, nor are they automatic reflexes resulting from contact with other varieties. The resilience and innovation we can see in contemporary Valdresmål are at odds with longer-term patterns – and this linguistic shift has happened at just the same time as broader cultural and ideological shifts. Analyzing the raw linguistic data out of context, we might not know what sense to make of the apparent-time changes discussed above. But in context, considering in-depth ethnographic data and local metalinguistic discourse, it is clear that dialect maintenance and change must be at least partly driven by both historic and recent language ideologies.

CHAPTER FIVE

A Must-Hear Attraction in the Nature and Culture Park

The central Norwegian district of Valdres has been a tourism destination since the turn of the twentieth century. In 1906, a rail line running north from Oslo was completed with its terminus in the small farming settlement of Fagernes, which has since become Valdres's commercial and administrative center. The railroad made travel between rural Valdres and the urban centers of Southern Norway much easier and more comfortable, and it provided Valdres residents with greater access to the goods, services, and opportunities available in the capital and beyond. The rail line, called *Valdresbanen* (the Valdres Railway), also quickly became popular with Norwegian urbanites, who were drawn to Valdres for its bucolic valleys and picturesque mountains, which flank the main farming and residential valleys to the north, west, and east. Construction of mountain hotels and other tourist facilities in Valdres followed the opening of Valdresbanen and the influx of travelers it carried on their way to take in striking views of pastoral landscapes, snow-capped peaks, and high-altitude lakes, along with the fresh air and recreational activities that were less available in the urban centers.

But they were not just there to experience nature, as the Norwegian countryside was also considered to be where the most "authentic" national culture could be found, in highly idealized and romantic ways (Hylland Eriksen 1993; Ween and Abram 2012), making it all the more important for urban residents to stay connected to rural places like

Valdres as regular visitors. Valdres and its natural landscapes have thus been "consumed" by nonlocals, both visually and through leisure recreation (Urry 1995, 2005), for well over a century, and place-based tourism development is far from a new phenomenon in the district. Today, Valdresbanen is no longer in operation, but a steady stream of domestic tourists continues to visit Valdres. Most Norwegian visitors come from urban areas, seeking experiences and vistas of mountain wilderness, as well as relaxation and recreational opportunities in a decidedly rural setting. Hiking and skiing in the kind of idyllic natural environments found in and around Valdres may even be understood as "central to the performance of nationalized urban identities" in Norway (Ween and Abram 2012, 160). Foreign tourists are also drawn to Valdres, and while they may enjoy its nature-based sights and activities, the district's venerable cultural institutions – the Valdres Folk Museum, established in 1901, and Valdres's six medieval wooden stave churches, constructed around 1160–1250 – are usually a greater priority for international visitors.

With the traditional, year-round economic base of farming in decline over the last generation, tourism has become more important than ever in Valdres, and vast public and private resources have been invested in tourism development, as is the case elsewhere in rural Norway (Forbord et al. 2012). In 2007, a coalition of politicians, public administrators, and members of the business community in Valdres came together in a concerted effort to market the region's various assets more effectively. Their intentions were both to grow Valdres's well-established tourist base and to attract new permanent residents to the area, which has experienced negative population growth for decades as young people leave for educational and work opportunities in more urban areas. This massive marketing campaign bestowed upon the rural district a new name, *Valdres Natur- og Kulturpark* (Valdres Nature and Culture Park) and a brand logo (see Figure 5.1), which both reflects and produces a new image of the valley. It is no longer just a rural district but now also promoted as a "park" open to visitors interested in experiences of rustic, traditional Norwegian nature and culture.

The Valdres Natur- og Kulturpark (VNK) project is explicitly about branding, and its leaders have aimed to make the district more recognizable and desirable as a destination for outsiders, as well as to create a stronger and more unified identity for Valdres and its residents.

Figure 5.1. Valdres Nature and Culture Park logo, 2018 updated version. Source: Valdres Natur- og Kulturpark.

VNK administrators recognize that long-term success for their project will necessitate convincing both potential visitors and life-long Valdres residents of the symbolic and material value of the district's natural and cultural resources. Since 2010, a primary VNK marketing scheme has focused on the richness of "sensorial" experiences available in Valdres, which the campaign also refers to as *Sanseriket Valdres* (Valdres, the Realm of Senses) in its documents, brochures, signage, and websites. Using the slogan *Valdres skjerper sansane* (Valdres heightens the senses), VNK marketing emphasizes what people can see, feel, taste, smell, and hear in their experiences of both the rural outdoors and cultural heritage in Valdres, and it has indeed contributed to more awareness, visibility, and economic viability for outdoor recreation and local "folk" traditions, from music and dance to artisanal food production, as well as the Valdres dialect.

The development of VNK's regional branding campaign has coincided closely with the revalorization of Valdresmål, and the two seem to work in tandem, each reinforcing the other. With its presently high value in the national linguistic marketplace (Bourdieu 1991), Valdresmål has become an important resource in tourism development in Valdres. The local dialect, or bits and pieces of it, have been put to use in print marketing, business names and signs, music and stage performances, hospitality encounters, and way-finding signage in towns and along hiking, skiing, and biking trails. Valdresmål's public presence has thus grown through recent tourism development, and its high symbolic value has been converted into economic capital, as the dialect and many of Valdres's other cultural resources are increasingly commodified.

The commodification of language, along with other forms of cultural heritage, has become common in the global era (Heller 2003; Duchêne and Heller 2012; Cavanaugh and Shankar 2014), but this particular case nevertheless has many interesting and unique features, not least in that it involves commodification of a non-normative, rural dialect. Dialect commodification in Valdres relies on pro-dialect ideologies, both national and local, for its effectiveness, and it contributes to the continuous process of re-enregisterment of the dialect, reproducing links to rural places, people, and products. Paradoxically, while commercial uses of the dialect certainly play a role in its revalorization, they also appear to be contributing to the kinds of selective linguistic maintenance discussed in Chapter 4, especially for those forms and features used most widely in marketing, leaving other pieces of Valdresmål behind in the process. This chapter examines where and how Valdresmål is used in marketing and tourism, showing that while the dialect remains vital, it has also been profoundly transformed – linguistically, socially, and ideologically – through revalorization and commodification in the twenty-first century.

SELLING NATURE AND CULTURE WITH DIALECT

In the summer of 2015, I accompanied a group of about a half-dozen people, aged twelve to over seventy, on a low-mountain trek in rural Valdres. Our mission that day was to post signs directing hikers with less intimate knowledge of the area to several places: a small mountain lake, called a *tjedn* in Valdresmål; a rather ordinary looking hill, locally described as a peak (*høgde*); and a small swimming hole at a bend in a stream. We carried with us the signs themselves, professionally produced, painted dark green with white letters, and with place names written in Valdresmål; more than a dozen fenceposts on which the signs were to be mounted; and a heavy iron rod, about a meter long with one pointed end for digging postholes and flat sides for pounding the posts into the ground.

We set out on a well-worn trail that starts uphill from an unpaved road, where there has long been a sign to the lake, which is a fishing destination marked on official maps as well. The lowest part of the trail runs along the edge of a summer mountain farm, or *støl*, that members of the signing party had family connections to and where they had spent significant amounts of time exploring the landscape and learning its important features from relatives in their parents' and grandparents' generations. They had used the lake for fishing and swimming, camped at its edge, and gathered cloudberries from the surrounding bogs. They had bathed in the creek's still, deep pool on warm summer days. And those who were alive while transhumant dairy farming was still in full swing had occasionally enjoyed the view from the peak while searching for errant cattle that failed to return in time for evening milking. Clearly these places were important to the group I hiked with and others with mountain farms in the immediate vicinity, but with intergenerational place-knowledge still flowing, why were we posting signs to identify these features in the natural landscape?

Among the group I accompanied was Olav, a gregarious self-studied local historian, who had taken it upon himself to request that these particular signs be produced. Olav was highly knowledgeable and cared deeply about the features and historic uses of the area around his family's *støl*, but he also had a long-simmering, mostly-friendly dispute with other local residents about which path was the "correct" one to get to the lake and which hill was properly called by the name on the signs we posted. So the new signs were intended to definitively mark the trail and the peak both for outsiders and for locals who may have had other ideas about these landscape features. But it was not just personal, as Olav's interests intersected with a large, public project focused on trail development, promotion, and branding.

The signs and fenceposts had been provided free of charge through a VNK-initiated program, the execution of which relied almost exclusively on the knowledge and labor of interested local volunteers. The aim, according to official VNK documents, was to produce uniform signage throughout Valdres as one component of a larger organizational goal to "become the best in Norway for hiking and skiing trails." The new signs were therefore intended to make some of Valdres's natural and cultural sites (and sights) more accessible for nonlocals, who may access outdoor recreational opportunities free of charge but also, in theory, make crucial contributions to the local economy through retail and hospitality spending.

Hundreds of these machine-made, dark green signs were posted throughout Valdres in the mid-2010s, sometimes replacing older, handmade ones, but just as often identifying places and trails that were previously unmarked, like the peak and swimming hole we signed. Crucially, almost all of the signs bear dialectal place-names, that is, the names of places and landscape features as they are known and talked about by local people in Valdresmål, which has led to an increased presence of the dialect in nature, even when local speakers are not in the vicinity. They are a critical component of Valdres's *linguistic landscape*, or "the language of public road signs, advertising, billboards, street names, place names, commercial shop signs, and public signs" (Landry and Bourhis 1997, 25), signaling links between dialect and territory and representing dominant values and ideologies of language and place more broadly (Leeman and Modan 2009). The proliferation of the new signs also contributes to a unified Valdres brand in its natural spaces, looking consistent and authoritative wherever they happen to pop up. The new signs certainly fulfill VNK's aim of aiding visitors in finding their way through unfamiliar terrain, but, in bearing dialectal place-names, they also do so in a way that injects local culture and language into the natural landscape, adding symbolic value to Valdres's already desirable scenery.

In Valdres's towns, villages, and along its roadways, the use of written dialect in marketing local businesses and products also grew substantially through the 2010s, in part through other projects spearheaded by VNK. This was by design, as "stimulat[ing] use of the Valdres dialect" was one of the twelve long-term strategies identified in VNK's initial ten-year plan (2007–17) for sustaining and developing Valdres's cultural heritage, a project consistently framed in terms of increasing economic profitability. Official encouragement to use Valdresmål thus contributes to the growing trend of using the "old" spoken dialect in new ways in written marketing, drawing on at-times romantic and nostalgic views of an imagined rural culture and past to position Valdres for a viable economic future.

Several local entrepreneurs in Valdres's central commercial district, the neighboring towns of Fagernes and Leira, have chosen Valdresmål names for their businesses in recent years, including Grepa Gøtt Café and designer clothing store Agalaust. *Grepa*, *gøtt*, and *agalaust* are all distinctly dialectal forms, and they are markedly non-normative. *Grepa* and *agalaust* are both positive, intensifying adjectives, like "really" or "super" in colloquial English, while *gøtt* means "good." These stores' signs and advertising, featuring non-normative written forms in large script, stand out among other businesses, where Bokmål and international brand names otherwise dominate. They serve to indicate that shops are locally owned, "add[ing] value to products that otherwise are hard to distinguish from one another," as Heller and McElhinny put it (2017, 248), and they are also a nod to pro-dialect ideologies and the pride locals have in Valdresmål and the district as a whole.

The use of dialect to express local pride was incorporated more explicitly in a large-scale VNK campaign begun in 2012 that marketed Valdres as a desirable destination using the catchphrase *Grepa stolt tå Valdres* (Very proud of Valdres). Here, both *grepa* (really/very) and *tå* (of) are distinctive and popularly recognizable Valdresmål forms, contrasting with regionally normative *veldig* and *av*. The Valdres pride campaign distributed hundreds of t-shirts, had a glossy website (unfortunately no longer accessible), and featured both local and national celebrities, often posing in the *Grepa stolt* t-shirt, who helped spread positive messages about Valdres in both online and print marketing. This is all very much in line with the widespread "pride and profit" framework identified by Duchêne and Heller (2012) that is broadly characteristic of linguistic and cultural commodification in late capitalism. It is noteworthy in this case, however, that "pride" may be interpreted as simultaneously both local and national, in that Valdres and other rural districts continue to function as primary sites of "traditional" Norwegian culture for the nation as a whole.

Capitalizing on local and national pride and recognizing its profitability, businesses throughout Valdres now use dialect in labeling and marketing for a variety of products. One place this has been especially prominent is for selling traditional local foods. As with signs marking popular trails and places in Valdres's more remote areas, handmade roadside signs have long advertised fresh homemade foods like *kurv*, a cured blood sausage, or *rumme*, sour cream, using dialectal forms, which contrast with normative *spekepølse* and *rømme*. But using Valdresmål in the main commercial districts and in more professional business marketing are relatively recent developments. For instance, Helle, a Valdres meat producer and former slaughterhouse operation, now labels its products with the slogan *Ekta gøtt!* (Really good!). Both words in the slogan are local forms, though easily recognizable to outsiders. *Ekta* corresponds to *ekte* in Bokmål and Nynorsk, while *gøtt* has its close counterpart in *godt* in both written norms. On their website, Leog Identity, the local design team behind the Helle labels notes that they are meant to represent "Valdres roots, traditions … authenticity, quality" for a relatively expensive and exclusive product that links Valdres's historic economic base of small-scale cattle farming to the newly profitable market for locally branded "artisanal" foods. Like the signs we posted for the mountain lake, swimming hole, and peak, the Helle slogan uses local language to "add value to experiences otherwise sold as being about something Romantic, whether natural or cultural, or both" (Heller and McElhinny 2017, 244).

In the summer of 2012, driving north along the E16 highway (Valdres's main traffic artery), which ultimately connects Oslo and Bergen, I spotted a highly unexpected example of written Valdresmål at a gas station. I insisted my spouse stop the car, even though we had American guests with us and were headed out of Valdres for sightseeing in the Western fjords that day. I simply had to take a picture of a large, professionally manufactured sign that read *Svøltin?* (Hungry?) and featured an image of a hamburger, available from the gas station's in-store grill (see Figure 5.2). The station was operated as a franchise of a major multinational brand, so it did not have a distinctly local name, nor, upon further investigation, did its convenience store sell traditional local products. But the single word on this new sign, hung from the pole holding up the main business sign, was markedly non-normative and dialectal. Like Helle's *Ekta gøtt!* slogan, *svøltin* is a written representation of spoken Valdresmål, and it does not conform to Bokmål or Nynorsk norms. The Bokmål form for "hungry" is *sulten*, while Nynorsk *svolten* is a bit closer to Valdresmål but still quite different to Norwegian ears, with both vowels being different. Aiming to stand out and attract tourists and travellers to fill up their tanks as well as their stomachs, the *Svøltin?* sign has garnered some quizzical but mostly positive attention. Indeed, a quick search for #svøltin on major social media platforms pulls up quite a few images of the sign, so I was not alone in being compelled to stop the car for a quick photo.

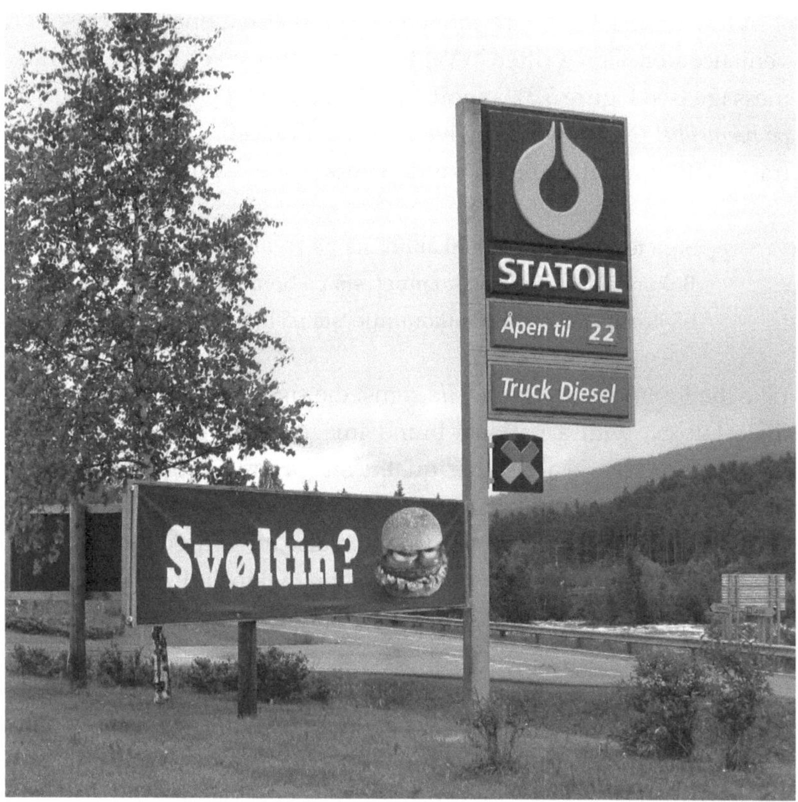

Figure 5.2. Gas station sign with text in Valdresmål: *Svøltin?* (Hungry?), summer 2012.

Clearly, the *Svøltin?* sign was a success. Driving past the station a few years later, in the summer of 2015, I found it replaced by an even larger version with a similar advertisement. The station had switched corporate brands, from Statoil to YX, and the new sign matched the new brand's look. One side of the updated version repeated the *Svøltin?* (Hungry?) message from the original sign, while the other side read *Møkjut bil?* (Dirty car?), inviting customers to use the on-site car wash. Like *svøltin*, the local form *møkjut* (dirty) has a similar-but-different corresponding form, *møkkete*, in Bokmål and Nynorsk, while *bil* is bivalent, that is, equally part of normative Norwegian varieties and Valdresmål, with no distinctly local alternative. Both *svøltin* and *møkjut* are therefore legible to nonlocal Norwegians, and the signs draw attention for their unexpected use of dialect in professional, public, written contexts.

A few years later, I encountered yet another national-franchise convenience store sign written in Valdresmål with an even more elaborated message (see Figure 5.3), announcing to drivers *No æ du framkåmin, stå på bremsidn!* (Now you've arrived, hit the brakes!). The linguistic contrasts with normative Bokmål and Nynorsk are readily observable:

> Sign text: No æ du framkåmin, stå på bremsidn!
> Bokmål: Nå er du fremkommet, stå på bremsene!
> Nynorsk: No er du framkom(m)e, stå på bremsane!

Like the *Svøltin?* and *Møkjut bil?* signs, the sign in Figure 5.3 combined dialectal text with a national brand image – the Joker grocery store logo, in this case – and other qualities of a professionally produced business sign. In contrast to the gas station signs, though, the Joker sign was situated along a mountain road and also advertised *lokalmat* (local food) available in the store, with a selection that includes Valdres-made meats, cheeses, baked goods, and beer. The store serves large numbers of recreational tourists during peak vacation periods and does good business offering up Valdres food culture in a location directly adjacent to prime hiking, fishing, and skiing opportunities in the Valdres mountains. And as with many other innovative uses of Valdresmål in Valdres's linguistic landscape, the store sign contributes to an impression of the district as quaintly rural and desirably distinctive.

Local businesses have been so effective in using dialect as a form of added value that at least one large, national corporation has also attempted to use Valdresmål to distinguish Valdres-related products in the crowded visual space of supermarkets. Tine, Norway's largest dairy company, has seasonally sold milk and cream exclusively from cows grazing in Valdres's mountains during the summer. Products labeled *Stølsfløyte* (cream from the mountain farm) and *Stølsmjølk* (milk from the mountain farm) from Tine have been sold in grocery stores in and outside of Valdres using dialect forms, as *støl* is the local word for a summer mountain farm, where cows traditionally graze openly (without fences) from late June to early September. Nationally, *seter* is the more common word for "mountain farm," found in both Bokmål and Nynorsk, though Nynorsk also allows *støl* as an acceptable variant. Nynorsk also includes *fløyte* and *mjølk* for "cream" and "milk," attesting to their relatively wide use beyond Valdres, while the most common

Figure 5.3. Convenience store sign with text in Valdres dialect, summer 2018.

forms, used in normative Bokmål, are *fløte* and *melk*. Remember Eva from Chapter 2, who adamantly claimed to only buy milk in cartons labeled *heilmjølk* (whole milk), because it was written in Nynorsk and thus linguistically and symbolically closer to Valdresmål? Many locals and visitors alike were also enthusiastic consumers of *stølsmjølk* and *stølsfløyte*, labeled with Valdresmål forms and bivalent with Nynorsk, making them thoroughly legitimate spellings, which lent authenticity and a traditional quality to these nationally branded products, thereby contributing to their economic profitability. As with the local products and scenery discussed above, Tine was able to convert a desire for rural culture and nature – cows grazing freely in idyllic mountain landscapes – into material capital.

SELLING DIALECT

When we got married in 2010, my spouse and I received several gifts of Valdres-related products from people we knew there, especially from folks who mostly knew us (or just me) as "interested in Valdres and dialect" professionally, rather than in more personal

Figure 5.4. Valdres dialect thermometer.

ways. Among these presents were fine local pottery, Valdres-related books, and an analog outdoor thermometer. The thermometer features a large, white, rectangular aluminum face and a mercury tube with temperature markings, ranging from −40 degrees to +50 degrees Celsius. It is an unremarkable household ware in every way, except that, in about a dozen places, the numerical temperature marks are accompanied by written descriptions, and these are in Valdresmål (see Figure 5.4). Around the mark for −15 degrees Celsius (+5 Fahrenheit), for example, it reads *"Grepa kaldt"* (Really cold), and, at just over 30 degrees Celsius (86 Fahrenheit), it proclaims "*Det gløsa gødt*," which does not lend itself as well to a literal translation in English but might be glossed as "It's good and fiery," with *gløsa* referring to the glowing of red-hot embers. In Bokmål and Nynorsk, the word *gløder* is used for "glows," equivalent in meaning to Valdresmål *gløsa*. The 30-degree marking also includes the oft-used dialect form *gødt* (good or well; sometimes spelled *gøtt*, as in the *Ekta gøtt!* slogan, with no difference in pronunciation), in contrast to normative *godt*.

This thermometer, which has come to hang on our porch at our home in Michigan, is as effective as any at indicating the temperature, but it was not really gifted to us for that purpose. Instead, it was designed to be sold and appreciated for the language printed on it. While dialect is increasingly used to sell nature, culture, and all sorts of products in Valdres, the thermometer is a commercial object that sells dialect, rather than the other way around. People buy it for the words printed on it much more than for its practical function, which has nothing specific to do with Valdres. While many of the words in this case are unique to Valdres, the phenomenon is not, as ethnographic linguists have also documented pieces of distinctive local dialects for sale on t-shirts, bumper stickers, magnets, and even jewelry in places like Pittsburgh (Johnstone 2013) and Michigan's Upper Peninsula (Remlinger 2017). In all of these places, enregistered dialects – local ways of speaking that people are highly aware of and talk a lot about – are such potent, recognizable symbols of the places they represent that their symbolic value has been converted quite directly into material, economic value. Dialects like Valdresmål, Pittsburghese, and Yooper (from Michigan's UP) are commodified not only through their use in commercial marketing but as real commodities in and of themselves.

Another large-scale Valdres Nature and Culture Park project has been to develop an array of popular festivals in Valdres, designed to bring large crowds and hospitality spending over long weekends. This festival-development strategy has been utilized for tourism and economic growth in many rural regions and small towns in Norway with variable results (Viken and Jaeger 2012), but in Valdres several music and food festivals that began as small, mostly local affairs in the pre-VNK era have become huge enterprises. One of these, Vinjerock, is a rock music festival that takes place high in Valdres's mountain wilderness, and its founders took it upon themselves in the festival's inaugural year to publish and sell a dialect dictionary. The *Vangsgjelding-Nynorsk Ordbok* (Vang Dialect-to-Nynorsk Dictionary) offered up a list of dialect words from Vang parish in northern Valdres, where Vinjerock is held, and provided festival attendees with translations in Nynorsk. Subtitled *Korleis Kommunisere med Dei Innfødte* (How to Communicate with the Natives), this was a decidedly humorous and highly elaborated dialect-selling commodity. And humor seems to be part of the appeal.

Like the dialect thermometer and the above examples of gas station signs, the Vinjerock dialect dictionary was funny partly because it used non-normative dialect in a venue generally reserved for "proper" writing, but also because it highlighted curious local words and linguistic features. For Norwegian speakers who have been thoroughly socialized into the heteroglossic national setting, where multiple varieties of Norwegian are constantly in contact and understanding non-normative dialects is generally expected, the dictionary was not really necessary as a tool for facilitating clear communication. Instead, it played on popular interest in and awareness of distinctive dialects like Valdresmål, including its northernmost variety, Vangsgjelding, contributing to their re-enregisterment and positive association with rural places, mountain landscapes, and traditional, authentic Norwegian culture. The thermometer, dictionary, and roadside signs featuring dialect allow reader-consumers the pleasure of recognizing and "decoding" non-normative written language, which is unusual and also out of place in professional commercial contexts, making them humorously pleasurable, as well, and all the more desirable and profitable in the rural retail marketplace.

CONSEQUENCES OF COMMODIFICATION

The use of Valdresmål in business names, signs, and other marketing has primarily been led by private businesses, but the public VNK organization has, in various ways, been supportive of dialect use in building a unified Valdres brand and identity since its inception. In an interview in the late 2000s, only a couple of years after the Valdres Nature and Culture Park concept had been established, I asked a senior administrator about the importance of dialect preservation and use in the context of VNK-led development efforts:

> *Det [dialektbruk] tru e e viktig og spesielt før uss som driv med merkevarebygging og valdresidentitet. Det e jo – der e dialekt en vesentlig del tå det. Men mø bygge jo identitet på mange måta med å bruke Vallers og eh, det e på en mate ein del i grunnverdia som – at mø ska på ein måte bygge Vallers tå – at alle forbind no positivt med det. Både gjennom kultur og natur og dialekt og litt forskjelligt.*
>
> It [dialect use] I think is important and especially for us working on branding and Valdres identity. It's – in those areas dialect is a significant part of it. But we're building identity in a lot of ways by using Vallers and uh, that's in a way a part of our foundational principles that – that we're going to sort of build Valdres out of – that everyone connects something positive to it [i.e., to Valdres]. Both through culture and nature and dialect and a variety of things.

As this VNK leader implies, people's positive impressions of the Valdres dialect contribute and are linked to positive associations with Valdres as a whole. And the central organizing principle he sketches – the idea that everyone should have positive associations with Valdres – continues to guide VNK projects and branding into the 2020s. Large-scale, professionally designed marketing campaigns, including *Valdres skjerper sansane* (Valdres heightens the senses) and *Grepa stolt tå Valdres* (Very proud of Valdres), have been among VNK's most visible promotional work in creating and selling positive associations. But district leaders have also engaged in many smaller-scale projects using a wide variety of strategies to promote the VNK brand and Valdres identity.

In talking to prominent artistic performers and athletes from Valdres, I learned that VNK administrators sometimes reached out to them personally, asking them to emphasize their Valdres roots in public appearances as a means of raising awareness of Valdres as a vital and desirable place. Local leaders wanted these high-profile Valdres natives to mention Valdres positively as often as possible, and they also specifically requested that local athletes and performers speak Valdresmål in media interviews and other appearances. In fact, as discussed in Chapter 3, most local celebrities-turned-Valdres-representatives were already committed dialect speakers, and Øystein, a performer and cultural entrepreneur, confessed to me that he had become irritated with VNK leaders' interest in milking his promotional potential. Beyond his personal annoyance, Øystein also worried about the longer-term consequences of exploiting local language, culture, and belonging in the pursuit of branding for economic gain:

> *Det bi litt voldsomt for uss scenekunstnere o idrettsutøvere ifrå Valdres […] Når mø prata Valdres o når mø øfto seie at mø e ifrå Valdres […] Når du då får politikere på nakkin so masa på at du ṣka seie <u>endå</u> meir at du e ifrå Valdres […] Men det e lurt å ikkji miste identiteten i merkevarebygging altså.*
>
> It gets to be a bit much for us stage performers and athletes from Valdres […] When we speak Valdres [dialect] and when we often say that we're from Valdres […] Then when you get politicians breathing down your neck and nagging that you should say even <u>more</u> that you're from Valdres […] But it's wise not to lose [our] identity in the branding process.

Øystein's concern with the prospect of Valdres *losing* its distinctive identity through branding was directly at odds with the VNK administrator quoted above, who told me the whole point of contemporary development efforts was to *build* a strong Valdres identity and brand. It seems that there is potential for both of these outcomes, and which might be more likely to prevail depends on what we look for and where.

From the outset, the Valdres Nature and Culture Park project has sought to promote Valdres nature and culture, including dialect, in order to forge a viable social and economic future. This is an ambitious undertaking and one that stems from an acknowledgment that Valdres's traditional rural lifestyle cannot provide enough income or opportunities for its current population in the twenty-first century. Family farming has not disappeared in Valdres, but it is in steep, probably irreversible decline, and one small farm can no longer support an entire family's economic needs. This has contributed to a slow but steady population decline over many decades, as young people have left for better opportunities elsewhere. But there are also many who want to stay in Valdres, where they have deep ancestral roots and ties to the land itself, and it is therefore with broad popular support that VNK has led the turn toward tourism, historically a secondary industry, as the last best hope going forward. As Pujolar and Jones have similarly observed in Catalonia, "one of the options left for those with attachments to territories of whatever kind is precisely to turn the territory into a commodity and make it into 'landscapes' or sites of 'memory,' that is, marketable objects for mobile consumers" (Pujolar and Jones 2012, 111).

Building on Valdres's established seasonal mountain tourism, the VNK plan has centered on now monetizing its abundant and distinctive rural resources: pastoral valley views, wild mountain landscapes, and "traditional" folk culture, including music, dance, art, and food, as well as many centuries-old wooden structures, from homes and barns to medieval churches. However, not every bit of local Valdres nature and culture is equally intriguing or desirable to outsiders, and so there is necessarily some selectivity in what is marketed and sold as representative of Valdres. Often those things that are most distinctive, and least familiar, are brought to the fore and presented as curiosities, beautiful perhaps, and worth paying for, but also far from most people's everyday realities. While many people do continue to participate in things like folk music and dance or make food by hand from raw, local ingredients, it is certainly not the case that most contemporary Valdres residents spend their days tending cattle and churning butter or their evenings dancing to fiddle music. As with speaking dialect, if they do any of those things, it is by self-conscious choice, as part of a thoroughly modern life and perspective that recognizes "traditional" Valdres culture and language as things that could easily disappear if not actively attended to.

This raises issues of *authenticity*, or people's perceptions of whether something is "real" or "true" or properly "traditional" and therefore valuable. But authenticity and tradition are always constructed (Hobsbawm and Ranger 1983; Lindholm 2008; Lau 2010; Cavanaugh and Shankar 2014), and they rely on shared knowledge, ideologies, and perceptions, learned through social interaction and discourse more broadly. Cultural objects and practices constructed as authentic are often believed to have come from an unbroken chain of tradition since time immemorial. However, historians and social scientists (along with many critical consumers) have long recognized that authentic, traditional culture is both flexible and frequently deployed strategically in capitalist marketplaces. In late 2006, initial plans and preparations for the Valdres Nature and Culture Park were coalescing, and local leaders brought in outside consultants for a seminar to advise and inspire. A visiting representative from a national business-and-culture organization encouraged Valdres politicians and entrepreneurs to focus on selling authentic (*ekte*) culture, and she also offered them a warning. "There can't be a hint of anything fake," she said, because "no one will buy that" (Skattebo 2006).

While many Valdres residents are proud of their local history, art forms, and foodways, old ways of doing things are readily dispensed with when innovative techniques and technologies make life easier, as is the case most everywhere. No one in Valdres milks an entire herd of cows by hand twice a day out of respect for cultural continuity or tradition. But they might happily demonstrate hand-milking to urban outsiders willing to pay for the experience (or at least buy some homemade cheese), and all involved can consider it to be both authentic and traditional, based on shared understandings of rural, peasant culture and its laudable status as the foundation of national and local identity in Norway and Valdres. So long as tourist-consumers' expectations are met, this is good business, but it also generally demands attention to details that contribute to authenticating the product or experience – for example, setting up a hand-split roundpole fence (*skigard*) around an old log storage building (*stabbur*) repurposed as a store, even though steel fencing and pole buildings are far more commonly used on working farms today. In contexts like these, speaking Valdres dialect and using Valdresmål on business signs and product labels are also critical tools for constructing authenticity. All of these things link back to a highly valued, imagined history, and they contribute to the construction of tradition and authenticity for tourist-consumers.

Through the years, Valdres business owners and VNK administrators have told me they see Valdresmål as an important source of added value for local products and tourist experiences, and they also, without exception, say they genuinely want the dialect to be preserved and used by future generations. Overwhelmingly, they see the prominent use of Valdresmål in marketing as something that contributes to its maintenance and continued use. If the dialect has high symbolic and economic value, they reason, then it is much more likely to persist. In some ways, this seems to be true, as commercial uses of Valdresmål have proliferated over the last decade in a fashion that would have been unimaginable in the late twentieth century. At the same time, however, these strategic uses of dialect in branding and marketing are usually quite brief – just a word or short phrase in Valdresmål, at most perhaps a sentence – and utilize a relatively small inventory of linguistic features.

Just as bits and pieces of local culture are carefully selected for presentation and sale to outsiders, a limited range of Valdresmål forms is used in most written marketing. Dialectal words for local food products are especially prominent, including *kurv* (a type of cured blood sausage), *rumme* (sour cream), and *rak(a)fisk* (trout that has been salted and allowed to ferment for several months). The first-person plural pronoun *mø* (we) and the adjectives *grepa* (very) and *gøtt* (good or well) are also used especially frequently, and it is common to see the Valdresmål definite plural articles *–adn*, *–idn*, and *–udn* (the-pl.). As the examples discussed earlier in this chapter show, many other distinctive words and phrases may be incorporated, but there are also limitations in terms of legibility that drive the selection of certain elements of Valdresmål as suitable for marketing and not others. If outsiders are unlikely to understand the message without further explanation, it will probably not be good marketing. Perhaps similarly, if a local custom is not interpreted as part of the "authentic," "traditional" culture, it cannot be easily sold in the touristic marketplace.

On the one hand, in this case and many others like it, we can see how such selective commodification and objectification can contribute to the erosion of complete, coherent, and variable linguistic and cultural systems, amplifying the very processes that valorization through commercialization was intended to interrupt. Simultaneously, however, those chunks of local language and culture that are selected for commercial use and public consumption may become both profitable and even more recognizable. "As cultural values and linguistic meanings are recruited into capitalist projects for their economic value," Cavanaugh and Shankar argue, the selective nature of this process "may also give them greater importance as social representations" (Cavanaugh and Shankar 2014, 61). This is to say that Valdres culture and dialect are not commodified intact or in their entirety; only parts of them are taken up and come to have economic value that, in turn, enhances their existing social and symbolic value. And it is most often those bits and pieces of local language and culture that are both legible to outsiders and perceived as "authentic" or "traditional" whose persistence can be ensured in an economy built on selling rural landscapes and life. These words and features are only part of a complete and grammatically coherent linguistic system, but they are central to what Valdresmål has become in the twenty-first century. In this way, commodification of language and culture may change the very things they are selling, as we can see Valdresmål being reshaped linguistically as well as economically in tourism development and adjacent commerce.

CHAPTER SIX

Finding the Local Past in a Global Future

Dialect in Valdres is different today than it was a generation or two ago. It has changed linguistically, with some older forms lost, others gaining ground, and new ones emerging. But even more profoundly, Valdresmål has changed culturally and ideologically, as it is put to different social and economic uses than in the past, producing new meanings in the process.

In the late 1990s, a local sociolinguist described Valdresmål as "*eit målføre i uføre*" (a dialect in disarray) (Kvåle 1999). Many people in Valdres at the time believed that local ways of speaking were on the verge of disappearing; that pessimistic assessment is still alive and well today. Older generations, especially, say that local youth no longer speak Vallers, or if they do it is "watered down," not like it is or was among their grandparents' and great-grandparents' generations. That young people in Valdres talk differently than their elders is plainly true, and it is an outcome of historic inequalities, as well as changing social, cultural, political, and economic circumstances, including increased geographic and social mobility. But we should always expect that linguistic systems will change in response to and in tandem with the new situations in which speakers find themselves, and Valdresmål is no exception.

Taking stock of the situation in the twenty-first century, it is abundantly clear that the Valdres dialect has not disappeared. Throughout this book, I have included and commented upon many young people in Valdres who use locally distinctive words and other linguistic features, and who identify as proud Valdresmål speakers. Most would also agree that they do not speak the dialect in the same way as their oldest relatives, and some of them wish they were more "fluent," for lack of a better word. Indeed, there is so much social pressure to maintain the local dialect that a few younger people told me they have even tried to practice with older dialect speakers in an effort to master some of the historic Vallers forms that were not used around them enough as young children to result in automatic acquisition. But it turns out that this can also be a frustrating process that ends in being told they still are not doing everything quite right when it comes to speaking Valdresmål "correctly." This kind of intergenerational conflict is far from unique in communities whose ancestral or heritage languages have changed, mixed, and lost parts as a result of social inequality or through shifting political or economic circumstances (Hill and Hill 1986; Heller and McElhinny 2017). Taking a critical perspective on intergenerational tensions around language, Avineri and Harasta observe that "language ideologies that insist upon unattainable standards for fluency can, intentionally or unintentionally, serve as handmaids of annihilation" (Avineri and Harasta 2021, 3). Thus, if researchers and speakers of Valdresmål want to understand the components and meaningfulness of local language in Valdres today, we might be better off paying attention to what contemporary dialect users *are* doing with their language, rather than focusing on differences from an idealized historic version of it.

The examples discussed and excerpted speech included in previous chapters show that plenty of locally distinctive linguistic forms are in regular use in Valdres today, both in everyday interactions, whether face-to-face or digitally mediated, and in the public and performative contexts of mass media and marketing. Locals and outsiders alike take pleasure in hearing and reading Valdresmål, and its high social and symbolic value is increasingly translated into economic gains for Valdres's hospitality and tourism-adjacent industries. In this context, Valdresmål has thus far persisted as a form of ordinary communication among locals who self-identify as dialect speakers, but it is also used and engaged with by many who do not consider themselves "fluent." People throughout Valdres have in common, though, an awareness of and appreciation for the local dialect, and in this way they are all part of what Avineri (2012) has termed a *metalinguistic community*, organized around language ideologies and practices that orient to Valdresmål as a cherished object of common heritage, rather than a more conventional *speech community*, bound to one another primarily through shared communicative patterns and norms (cf. Morgan 2015). This is one way in which Valdresmål has changed socially, and it opens up new possibilities for connection around the dialect for long-term residents, newcomers, and visitors alike.

Most people in Valdres whose families have ancestral roots there do still speak in ways that are highly distinctive, and Valdresmål can still be understood as a prototypical geographic dialect used in local interactional contexts. Today, many Valdresmål speakers also use the dialect in interactions with speakers of normative Norwegian and in relatively formal contexts, including national media appearances, expecting (at times perhaps insisting) that outsiders will understand and appreciate Vallers. Beyond interactional speech, however, the Valdres dialect is also conceptualized as cultural heritage (*kulturarv*): it is also "words and names, promotional materials, plays, and songs," and people are connected to it through emotion and nostalgia, as well as ordinary use (Avineri and Harasta 2021, 3). In these more metalinguistic, objectified forms, Valdresmål does indeed seem to be secure for the foreseeable future, even as it is true that some historic features have been lost and others are falling out of regular use due to intense sociolinguistic contact and population mobility. As with so many other minoritized languages, dialects, and ways of speaking, long-term social and economic pressures have led to linguistic shift, but the words, names, and other pieces that are retained may still serve as valuable links to the past and places in Valdres that people hold dear and wish to remember.

Valdres is a "small" and relatively peripheral community in geographic and social terms, but it is nevertheless caught up and embedded in larger national and global systems. National culture and identity formations in Norway have consistently constructed small, rural communities and mountain wilderness, like those found in Valdres, as part of a common heritage and past shared by all ethnic Norwegians. In large measure, this is what has made Valdres an attractive tourism destination for over a century. Interest in "traditional" Norwegian landscapes and culture, including its varied dialects, has also grown considerably in recent decades, buoyed as well by more global trends of appreciation for discernably "local," "authentic," and "artisanal" products and experiences in the late-capitalist sea of mass-produced, globally sourced, blandly generic things for sale.

This has worked out well for Valdres and Valdresmål thus far, as the district was able to successfully position itself as a premier national tourism destination by the late 2010s. Today, in order to grow tourism and cultural production in Valdres going forward, local officials and developers are increasingly looking beyond Norway's population of just over five million. But targeting a more diverse audience will require new strategies to produce meaningful experiences for international visitors, especially those from beyond Scandinavia and Europe, whose ideas of "traditional" and "authentic" Norwegian culture are necessarily different. Linguistically, Valdresmål is of little use in selling Valdres and Norwegian culture to a more global tourist base, as "performances have to have an audience speaking the same language … in order to maintain the full force of linguistic authentication" (Heller and Duchêne 2012, 11). Valdresmål cannot add value if visitors do not recognize it as local, distinctive, or traditional.

As I have talked to people about Valdresmål over the last fifteen years or so, asking about the future of the dialect has most often brought negative, if resigned, assessments that it will not last much longer. Most people agree that Bokmål and *bymål* (city language) will eventually be more commonly used than the Valdres dialect within the district. In an early interview from 2007, however, a local entrepreneur suggested to me that the biggest threat to Valdresmål was not normative Norwegian. "Oh really?" I asked. "What then?" "English," he told me, "English is what will win out in the end." This has not yet transpired, and I have no expectation that English will displace Norwegian in everyday life in Valdres or elsewhere in Norway any time soon. But within a more international future for the Valdres tourism industry, Vallers is likely to be displaced not by more normative forms of Norwegian, which is itself a small language in global terms, but indeed by English, a language that is already widely spoken and taught from the earliest grades in Norway, as it is in so many other places, for its global economic and political value. Observing local linguistic practice today, it is also true that mixing Valdresmål and English is increasingly common, and this speaks to the intersecting local and global systems of value that contemporary Valdres residents must navigate. While most have deep attachments to the district, many are also intrigued by opportunities much farther afield, especially when it comes to education and work.

Without a stable population, Valdres and its language and culture would of course struggle to survive, and so the ultimate goal of economic redevelopment has not been to entertain visitors but to make it possible for people to continue to provide for themselves in a globalized economy that has slowly but surely reshaped life in rural, out-of-the-way places like Valdres just as much as anywhere else. Ordinary people and local leaders alike are keenly aware of Valdres's global geographic, cultural, and linguistic peripherality, but they also have an unwavering desire to see their community continue to thrive. Forging a creative path forward, they have self-consciously reinvented local linguistic and cultural traditions, putting them to new uses and transforming them both practically and ideologically in the process. There are always more changes and challenges ahead, but recent creative and entrepreneurial efforts have demonstrated the resilience and capacity for innovation necessary for small communities to thrive in an increasingly globalized world.

Appendix A: Transcription Conventions

Transcription conventions used in the text are adapted from established conversation- and discourse-analytic practice.

:	A colon indicates an extended or elongated sound. Multiple colons indicate further elongation.
–	A dash indicates an abrupt cutoff.
____	Underlining indicates word or syllable emphasis.
CAPS	Words in all capital letters indicated raised volume.
@	An "at" symbol indicates laughter. One @ is equivalent to one laughter pulse.
[	Open square brackets indicate overlapping utterances and occur at the start of an overlap.
[ ]	Closed square brackets indicate transcriber clarifications where this is helpful for reader understanding.
[...]	A series of three close periods in square brackets indicates talk omitted from the transcript.
,	A comma indicates a brief pause.
.	A period with spaces around it indicates a significant unmeasured pause. Each period is roughly equivalent to a one-second pause.

All unconventional spellings are loosely phonetic according to the general orthographic norms of Norwegian.

Appendix B: Glossary of Linguistic Terms

accusative case the grammatical case used for a noun or pronoun when it is (1) the direct object of a verb (action), (2) the object of a preposition that always requires accusative forms, or (3) the object of a dual-case preposition when direction or movement is indicated

dative case the grammatical case used for a noun or pronoun when it is (1) the indirect object of a verb (action), (2) the object of a preposition that always requires dative forms, or (3) the object of a dual-case preposition when location is indicated

dative preposition one of a class of prepositions that either always requires dative-case noun forms or requires them when location is indicated

diphthong a sound formed by combining two single vowel sounds in a single syllable

direct object a noun that is the recipient of an action (verb)

F0, or fundamental frequency a periodic sound wave in speech heard as pitch

F1, or first formant a periodic sound wave in speech related to vowel height; lower Hz values correspond to "high" vowels and vice versa

F2, or second formant a periodic sound wave in speech related to vowel front-ness/back-ness; lower Hz correspond to "back" vowels and vice versa

indirect object a noun that is affected by an action (verb), but not the primary object of the action

lexicon the words of a given language

monophthong a single vowel sound

morpheme a meaningful unit of language, whether a word that cannot be further divided or a portion of a word that carries part of its meaning

morphology the study of the structure of words and their meaningful parts

nominative case the grammatical case for a noun or pronoun when it is the subject of a sentence

phonetics the study of speech sounds

phonology the system of speech sounds and their contrasts within a given language

References

Aars, Ivar. 1963. "Substantiv i Nord-Aurdal: Oppland." Hovedfag thesis, University of Oslo.

Aasen, Ivar. (1842–81) 2002. *Ord, Uttrykk og Inntrykk frå Hallingdal og Valdres*. Ål: Boksmia Forlag.

Agha, Asif. 2007. *Language and Social Relations*. Cambridge: Cambridge University Press.

———. 2011. "Meet Mediatization." *Language & Communication* 31(3): 163–70. https://doi.org/10.1016/j.langcom.2011.03.006.

Anderson, Benedict. 1991. *Imagined Communities: Reflections on the Origin and Spread of Nationalism*. London: Verso.

Auer, Peter, Frans Hinskens, and Paul Kerswill, eds. 2005. *Dialect Change: Convergence and Divergence in European Languages*. Cambridge: Cambridge University Press.

Avineri, Netta. 2012. "Heritage Language Socialization Practices in Secular Yiddish Educational Contexts: The Creation of a Metalinguistic Community." PhD diss., University of California Los Angeles.

Avineri, Netta, and Jesse Harasta, eds. 2021. *Metalinguistic Communities: Case Studies of Agency, Ideology, and Symbolic Uses of Language*. Palgrave Macmillan.

Bakhtin, Mikhail. 1981. *The Dialogic Imagination*. Austin: University of Texas Press.

———. 1984. *Problems of Dostoevsky's Poetics*. Minneapolis: University of Minnesota Press.

Baugh, John. 1992. "Hypocorrection: Mistakes in Production of Vernacular African American English as a Second Dialect." *Language and Communication* 12(3/4): 317–26. https://doi.org/10.1016/0271-5309(92)90019-6.

Beito, Olav T. 1959. "Valdresmålet." In *Valdres Bygdebok*, Vol. 2, edited by Knut Hermundstad, 231–94. Fagernes: Valdres Historielag.

———. 1979. *Artiklar og Taler i Utval*. Oslo: Universitetsforlaget.

Bell, Allan. 1984. "Language Style as Audience Design." *Language in Society* 13(2): 145–204. https://doi.org/10.1017/S004740450001037X.

Berge Rudi, Nina. 2007. "Språkvariasjonar i To Dalføre: Ei Sosiolingvistisk Gransking av Talemålet blant 18-20-Åringar i Hallingdal og Gudbrandsdalen." MA thesis, University of Oslo.

Blom, Jan-Petter, and John J. Gumperz. 1972. "Social Meaning in Linguistic Structure: Codeswitching in Norway." In *Directions in Sociolinguistics: The Ethnography of Speaking*, edited by John J. Gumperz and Dell Hymes, 407–32. New York: Holt, Reinhart, and Winston.

Boersma, Paul, and David Weenink. 2008. Praat, Version 5.0.27 for Mac OS X. http://www.praat.org.

Bourdieu, Pierre. 1991. *Language and Symbolic Power*. Cambridge, MA: Harvard University Press.

Bucken-Knapp, Gregg. 2003. *Elites, Language, and the Politics of Identity: The Norwegian Case in Comparative Perspective*. Albany: SUNY Press.

Carrera-Sabaté, Josefina. 2006. "Some Connections Between Linguistic Change and the Written Language: The Behavior of Speakers Aged 3 to 20." *Language Variation and Change* 18(1): 15–34. https://doi.org/10.1017/S0954394506060017.

Cavanaugh, Jillian R. 2009. *Living Memory: The Social Aesthetics of Language in a Northern Italian Town*. Malden, MA: Wiley Blackwell.

Cavanaugh, Jillian R., and Shalini Shankar. 2014. "Producing Authenticity in Global Capitalism: Language, Materiality, and Value." *American Anthropologist* 116(1): 51–64. https://doi.org/10.1111/aman.12075.

Chambers, J.K. 1988. "Acquisition of Phonological Variants." In *Methods in Dialectology*, edited by Alan R. Thomas, 650–65. Clevedon: Multilingual Matters.

Coupland, Nikolas, and Hywel Bishop. 2007. "Ideologised Values for British Accents." *Journal of Sociolinguistics* 11(1): 74–93. https://doi.org/10.1111/j.1467-9841.2007.00311.x.

Duchêne, Alexandre, and Monica Heller, eds. 2012. *Language and Late Capitalism: Pride and Profit*. New York: Routledge.

Eckert, Penelope. 2004. "Adolescent Language." In *Language in the USA*, edited by Edward Finegan and John R. Rickford, 361–74. Cambridge: Cambridge University Press.

Ervin-Tripp, Susan. 2001. "Variety, Style-Shifting, and Ideology." In *Style and Sociolinguistic Variation*, edited by Penelope Eckert and John R. Rickford, 44–56. New York: Cambridge University Press.

Forbord, Magnus, Gunn-Turid Kvam, and Martin Rønningen, eds. 2012. *Turisme i Distriktene*. Trondheim: Tapir.

Fridland, Valerie, and Kathryn Bartlett. 2006. "Correctness, Pleasantness, and Degree of Difference Ratings Across Regions." *American Speech* 81(4): 358–86. https://doi.org/10.1215/00031283-2006-025.

Gal, Susan, and Judith T. Irvine. 2019. *Signs of Difference: Language and Ideology in Social Life*. Cambridge: Cambridge University Press.

Haugen, Einar. 1966. *Language Conflict and Language Planning: The Case of Modern Norway*. Cambridge, MA: Harvard University Press.

———. 1972. *The Ecology of Language*. Stanford: Stanford University Press.

Haugen, Ragnhild. 2004. "Språk og Språkhaldningar hjå Ungdomar i Sogndal." PhD diss., University of Bergen.

Heller, Monica. 2003. "Globalization, the New Economy and the Commodification of Language and Identity." *Journal of Sociolinguistics* 7(4): 473–92. https://doi.org/10.1111/j.1467-9841.2003.00238.x.

Heller, Monica, and Alexandre Duchêne. 2012. "Pride and Profit: Changing Discourses of Language, Capital, and Nation-State." In *Language in Late Capitalism*, edited by Alexandre Duchêne and Monica Heller, 1–21. London: Routledge.

Heller, Monica, and Bonnie McElhinny. 2017. *Language, Capitalism, Colonialism: Toward a Critical History*. Toronto: University of Toronto Press.

Hernández-Campoy, Juan Manuel, and Juan Antonio Cutillas-Espinosa. 2012. "Style-Shifting Revisited." In *Style-Shifting in Public: New Perspectives on Stylistic Variation*, edited by J.M. Hernández-Campoy and J.A. Cutillas-Espinosa, 1–18. Amsterdam: John Benjamins.

Hill, Jane H. 1995. "The Voices of Don Gabriel: Responsibility and Self in a Modern Mexicano Narrative." In *The Dialogic Emergence of Culture*, edited by Dennis Tedlock and Bruce Mannheim, 97–147. Champaign, IL: University of Illinois Press.

———. 2008. *The Everyday Language of White Racism*. Malden, MA: Wiley-Blackwell.

Hill, Jane H., and Kenneth C. Hill. 1986. *Speaking Mexicano: Dynamics of Syncretic Language in Central Mexico*. Tucson: University of Arizona Press.

Hilton, Nanna Haug. 2010. "Regional Dialect Levelling and Language Standards: Changes in the Hønefoss Dialect." PhD thesis, University of York.

Hobsbawm, Eric, and Terrence Ranger, eds. 1983. *The Invention of Tradition*. New York: Cambridge University Press.

Holmes, Janet, and Paul Kerswill. 2008. "Contact Is Not Enough: A Response to Trudgill." *Language in Society* 37(2): 273–77. https://doi.org/10.1017/S0047404508080342.

Hylland Eriksen, Thomas. 1993. "Being Norwegian in a Shrinking World: Reflections on Norwegian Identity." In *Continuity and Change: Aspects of Contemporary Norway*, edited by Anne C. Kiel, 11–37. Oxford: Scandinavian University Press.

Irvine, Judith T. 1989. "When Talk Isn't Cheap: Language and Political Economy." *American Ethnologist* 16(2): 248–67. https://doi.org/10.1525/ae.1989.16.2.02a00040.

———. 1990. "Registering Affect: Heteroglossia in the Linguistic Expression of Emotion." In *Language and the Politics of Emotion*, edited by Catherine Lutz and Lila Abu-Lughod, 126–61. New York: Cambridge University Press.

Irvine, Judith T., and Susan Gal. 2000. "Language Ideology and Linguistic Differentiation." In *Regimes of Language: Ideologies, Polities, and Identities*, edited by Paul V. Kroskrity, 35–83. Santa Fe: SAR.

Jaffe, Alexandra. 1999. *Ideologies in Action: Language Politics on Corsica*. Berlin: Mouton de Gruyter.

Jahr, Ernst Håkon. 1984. *Talemålet i Skolen. En Studie av Drøftninger og Bestemmelser om Muntlig Språkbruk i Folkeskolen (fra 1874 til 1925)*. Oslo: Novus.

———. 2014. *Language Planning as a Sociolinguistic Experiment: The Case of Modern Norwegian*. Edinburgh: Edinburgh University Press.

Jahr, Ernst Håkon, and Karol Janicki. 1995. "The Function of the Standard Variety: A Contrastive Study of Norwegian and Polish." *International Journal of the Sociology of Language* 115: 25–45. https://doi.org/10.1515/ijsl.1995.115.25.

Jenshus, Gunnar. 1986. *Fronsmålet (The Fron Dialect)*. Vinstra: Fron Historielag.

Johnstone, Barbara. 2009. "Pittsburghese Shirts: Commodification and the Enregisterment of an Urban Dialect." *American Speech* 84(2): 157–75. https://doi.org/10.1215/00031283-2009-013.

———. 2013. *Speaking Pittsburghese: The Story of a Dialect*. New York: Oxford University Press.

Keane, Webb. 2003. "Semiotics and the Social Analysis of Material Things." *Language and Communication* 23(3–4): 409–25. https://doi.org/10.1016/S0271-5309(03)00010-7.

Kerswill, Paul. 2003. "Dialect Levelling and Geographical Diffusion in British English." In *Social Dialectology: In Honour of Peter Trudgill*, edited by David Britain and Jenny Cheshire, 223–43. Amsterdam: John Benjamins.

Kolsrud, Sigurd. (1921) 1979. "Kringum Maalskiftet." In *Fra Norsk Språkhistorie: En Antologie*, 2nd ed., edited by Eskil Hanssen, 54–79. Oslo: Universitetsforlaget.

Kristiansen, Tore, and Lars S. Vikør. 2006. "Nordiske Språkhaldningar—Jamføring og Konklusjonar." In *Nordiske Språkhaldningar: Ei Meiningsmåling*, edited by Tore Kristiansen and Lars S. Vikør, 199–214. Oslo: Novus.

Kristoffersen, Gjert. 2000. *The Phonology of Norwegian*. Cambridge: Oxford University Press.

Kvåle, Karen Marie. 1999. "Eit Målføre i Uføre: Talemålsendring i Valdres." Hovedfag thesis, University of Oslo.
Labov, William. 1963. "The Social Motivation of a Sound Change." *Word* 19: 273–309. https://doi.org/10.1080/00437956.1963.11659799.
———. 1972. *Sociolinguistic Patterns*. Philadelphia: University of Pennsylvania Press.
———. 1994. *Principles of Linguistic Change: Internal Factors*, Vol. 1. Malden, MA: Blackwell.
Labov, William, Malcah Yaeger, and Richard Steiner. 1972. *A Quantitative Study of Sound Change in Progress*. Philadelphia: US Regional Survey.
Landry, Rodrigue, and Richard Y. Bourhis. 1997. "Linguistic Landscape and Ethnolinguistic Vitality: An Empirical Study." *Journal of Language and Social Psychology* 16(1): 23–49.
Lau, Raymond W.K. 2010. "Revisiting Authenticity: A Social Realist Approach." *Annals of Tourism Research* 37(2): 478–98.
Leeman, Jennifer, and Gabriella Modan. 2009. "Commodified Language in Chinatown: A Contextualized Approach to Linguistic Landscape." *Journal of Sociolinguistics* 13(3): 332–62.
Lindholm, Charles. 2008. *Culture and Authenticity*. Malden, MA: Blackwell.
Lundeby, Einar, and Ingvald Torvik. 1956. *Språket Vårt gjennom Tidene: Kort Norsk Språkhistorie*. Oslo: Gyldendal.
Mæhlum, Brit. 1996. "Codeswitching in Hemnesberget – Myth or Reality?" *Journal of Pragmatics* 25(6): 749–61. https://doi.org/10.1016/0378-2166(95)00027-5.
———. 2009. "Standardtalemål? Naturligvis! En Argumentasjon for Eksistensen av et Norsk Standardtalemål." *Norsk Lingvistisk Tidsskrift* 27(1): 7–26.
Mæhlum, Brit Kirsten, and Stian Hårstad. 2018. "Nasjonale og Regionale Identiteter." In *Norsk Språkhistorie III: Ideologi*, edited by Helge Sandøy, Agnete Nesse, and Tove Bull, 245–326. Oslo: Novus.
Mæhlum, Brit, and Unn Røyneland. 2009. "Dialektparadiset Norge—En Sannhet med Modifikasjoner." In *I Mund og Bog: 25 artikler*, edited by Henrik Hovmark, Iben Stampe Sletten, and Asgerd Gudiksen, 219–31. Copenhagen: Museum Tusculanum.
———. 2018. "Dialekt, Indeksikalitet og Identitet. Tilstandsrapport fra Provinsen." In *Dansk til det 21. Århundrede—Sprog og Samfunn*, edited by Tanya K. Christensen, Christina Fogtmann, Torben Juel Jensen, Martha Sif Karrebæk, Marie Mægaard, Nicolai Pharao, and Pia Quist, 247–61. Copenhagen: U Press.
Mendoza-Denton, Norma. 1999. "Style." *Journal of Linguistic Anthropology* 9(1/2): 238–40. https://doi.org/10.1525/jlin.1999.9.1-2.238.
Moe, Moltke. 1909. "Nationalitet og Kultur." *Samtiden* 20: 17–28.
Morgan, Marcyliena. 2015. *Speech Communities*. Cambridge: Cambridge University Press.

Nesse, Agnete. 2015. "Bruk av Dialekt og Standardtalemål i Offentligheten i Norge etter 1800." In *Talemål etter 1800. Norsk i Jamføring med Andre Nordiske Språk*, edited by Helge Sandøy, 89–111. Oslo: Novus.
Niedzielski, Nancy A., and Dennis R. Preston. 2000. *Folk Linguistics*. Berlin: Mouton de Gruyter.
Noregs Mållag. 2021. "Medlemsrekord for Mållaget!" https://www.nm.no/medlemsrekord-for-mallaget/.
Pedersen, Inge Lise. 2005. "Processes of Standardisation in Scandinavia." In *Dialect Change: Convergence and Divergence in European Languages*, edited by Peter Auer, Frans Hinskens, and Paul Kerswill, 171–95. Cambridge: Cambridge University Press.
Preston, Dennis R. 1989. *Perceptual Dialectology: Nonlinguists' Views of Areal Linguistics*. Dordrecht: Foris.
———. 1999. *A Handbook of Perceptual Dialectology*, Vol. 1. Amsterdam: John Benjamins.
Pujolar, Joan. 2006. *Language, Culture and Tourism: Perspectives in Barcelona and Catalonia*. Barcelona: Turisme de Barcelona.
Pujolar, Joan, and Kathryn Jones. 2012. "Literary Tourism: New Appropriations of Landscape and Territory in Catalonia." In *Language and Late Capitalism: Pride and Profit*, edited by Alexandre Duchêne and Monica Heller, 93–115. Routledge.
Remlinger, Kathryn A. 2017. *Yooper Talk: Dialect as Identity in Michigan's Upper Peninsula*. Madison: University of Wisconsin Press.
Røyneland, Unn. 2005. "Dialektnivellering, Ungdom og Identitet, Ein Komparativ Studie av Språkleg Variasjon og Endring i To Tilgrensande Dialektområde, Røros og Tynset." PhD diss., University of Oslo.
———. 2009. "Dialects in Norway: Catching Up with the Rest of Europe?" *International Journal of the Sociology of Language* 196/197: 7–30. https://doi.org/10.1515/IJSL.2009.015.
———. 2020. "Regional Varieties in Norway Revisited." In *Intermediate Language Varieties: Koinai and Regional Standards in Europe*, edited by Massimo Cerutti and Stavroula Tsiplakou, 31–54. Amsterdam: John Benjamins.
Sandøy, Helge. 1998. "The Diffusion of a New Morphology in Norwegian Dialects." *Folia Linguistica* 32(1–2): 83–100. https://doi.org/10.1515/flin.1998.32.1-2.83.
———. 2009. "Standardtalemål i Norge? Ja, men …!" *Norsk Lingvistisk Tidsskrift* 27(1): 27–47.
———. 2011. "Language Culture in Norway: A Tradition of Questioning Language Standard Norms." In *Standard Languages and Language Standards in a Changing Europe*, edited by Tore Kristiansen and Nikolas Coupland, 119–26. Oslo: Novus.
———. 2015. "Austlandsk etter 1800." In *Talemål etter 1800. Norsk i Jamføring med Andre Nordiske Språk*, edited by Helge Sandøy, 159–80. Oslo: Novus.

Sankoff, David, Sali A. Tagliamonte, and Eric Smith. 2005. *Goldvarb X: A Variable-Rule Application for Macintosh and Windows*. http://individual.utoronto.ca/tagliamonte/Goldvarb/GV_index.htm.

Schilling-Estes, Natalie. 1998. "Investigating 'Self-Conscious' Speech: The Performance Register in Ocracoke English." *Language in Society* 27: 53–83.

Seip, Didrik Arup. (1955) 1979. "Fra Norsk Språkhistorie til Omkring 1370." In *Fra Norsk Språkhistorie: En Antologi*, 2nd ed., edited by Eskil Hanssen, 25–53. Oslo: Universitetsforlaget.

Silverstein, Michael. 2003. "Indexical Order and the Dialectics of Sociolinguistic Life." *Language and Communication* 23(3–4): 193–229. https://doi.org/10.1016/S0271-5309(03)00013-2.

Skard, Vemund. 1976. *Norsk Språkhistorie, Bind 1: Til 1523*. Oslo: Universitetsforlaget.

Skattebo, Geir Helge. 2006. "Står saman om Merkevaren." *Avisa Valdres*, November 16, 2006.

Sollid, Hilde. 2014. "Hierarchical Dialect Encounters in Norway." *Acta Borealia* 31(2): 111–30. https://doi.org/10.1080/08003831.2014.967969.

Spitulnik, Debra. 1999. "Media." *Journal of Linguistic Anthropology* 9(1/2): 148–51. https://doi.org/10.1525/jlin.1999.9.1-2.148.

Statistikk Sentralbyrå. 2009. "Kulturstatistikk 2008, Tabell 14.7: Norsk rikskringkasting: Sendetid i radio og fjernsyn, etter målform, 2003–2008." Accessed January 10, 2010. http://www.ssb.no/nos_kultur/nos_d429/tab/14.7.html.

Stokstad, Ingunn. 2007. "Talemål og Livsverd: Ein Aldersavgrensa Populasjonsstudie blant Ungdomar i Aurland i Sogn (Spoken Language and Lifeworld: An Age-delimited Population Study among Youth in Aurland Parish in Sogn Fylke)." MA thesis, University of Bergen.

Strand, Thea R. 2009. "Varieties in Dialogue: Dialect Use and Change in Rural Valdres, Norway." PhD diss., University of Arizona.

———. 2012a. "Dialect as Style in Norwegian Mass Media." In *Style-Shifting in Public: New Perspectives on Stylistic Variation*, edited by Juan Manuel Hernández-Campoy and Juan Antonio Cutillas-Espinosa, 185–203. Amsterdam: John Benjamins.

———. 2012b. "Winning the Dialect Popularity Contest: Mass-Mediated Language Ideologies and Local Responses in Rural Valdres, Norway." *Journal of Linguistic Anthropology* 22(1): 23–43. https://doi.org/10.1111/j.1548-1395.2012.01116.x.

———. 2015. "Pro-dialect Practices and Linguistic Commodification in Rural Valdres, Norway." In *Language Variation – European Perspectives V*, edited by Eivind N. Torgersen, Stian Hårstad, Brit Mæhlum, and Unn Røyneland, 211–23. Amsterdam: John Benjamins.

———. 2019. "Tradition as Innovation: Dialect Revalorization and Maximal Orthographic Distinction in Rural Norwegian Writing." *Multilingua* 38(1): 51–68. https://doi.org/10.1515/multi-2018-0006.

Swinehart, Karl F. 2008. "The Mass-Mediated Chronotope, Radical Counterpublics, and Dialect in 1970s Norway: The Case of Vømmøl Spellmanslag." *Journal of Linguistic Anthropology* 18(2): 290–301. https://doi.org/10.1111/j.1548-1395.2008.00023.x.

Thoengen, Vigdis. 1994. "Hallingmål eller Bokmål? En Talemålsundersøkelse blant Skolebarn i Nes i Hallingdal." MA thesis, University of Oslo.

Thomas, Erik R., and Tyler Kendall. 2007. "NORM: The Vowel Normalization and Plotting Suite." http://ncslaap.lib.ncsu.edu/tools/norm.

Urry, John. 1995. *Consuming Places*. London: Routledge.

———. 2005. "The 'Consuming' of Place." In *Discourse, Communication, and Tourism*, edited by Adam Jaworski and Annette Pritchard, 19–27. Clevedon: Channel View.

Venås, Kjell. 1977. *Hallingmålet*. Oslo: Det Norske Samlaget.

Viken, Arvid, and Kari Jæger. 2012. "Festivalisering av Bygde-Norge – Lokalsamfunnsutvikling Ispedd Turisme." In *Turisme i Distriktene*, edited by Magnus Forbord, Gunn-Turid Kvam, and Martin Rønningen, 211–30. Trondheim: Tapir.

Vikør, Lars. 1993. *The Nordic Languages: Their Status and Interrelations*. Oslo: Novus.

Wangensteen, Bøye. 1971. "Skilnader i Ordtilfanget i Vangsmålet hjå Eldre og Yngre." Hovedfag thesis, University of Oslo.

Ween, Gro, and Simone Abram. 2012. "The Norwegian Trekking Association: Trekking as Constituting the Nation." *Landscape Research* 37(2): 155–71. https://doi.org/10.1080/01426397.2011.651112.

Woolard, Kathryn A. 1998. "Simultaneity and Bivalency as Strategies in Bilingualism." *Journal of Linguistic Anthropology* 8(1): 3–29. https://doi.org/10.1525/jlin.1998.8.1.3.

———. 2008. "Why *Dat* Now? Linguistic-Anthropological Contributions to the Explanation of Sociolinguistic Icons and Change." *Journal of Sociolinguistics* 12(4): 432–52. https://doi.org/10.1111/j.1467-9841.2008.00375.x.

Woolard, Kathryn A., and Bambi B. Schieffelin. 1994. "Language Ideology." *Annual Review of Anthropology* 23: 55–82. https://doi.org/10.1146/annurev.an.23.100194.000415.

Wroblewski, Michael. 2021. *Remaking Kichwa: Language and Indigenous Pluralism in Amazonian Ecuador*. London: Bloomsbury.

Index

Page numbers in italics indicate illustrations. Page numbers in bold indicate definitions.

TC TEACHING CULTURE

Ethnographies for the Classroom

Editor: John Barker, University of British Columbia

This series is an essential resource for instructors searching for ethnographic case studies that are contemporary, engaging, provocative, and created specifically with undergraduate students in mind. Written with clarity and personal warmth, books in the series introduce students to the core methods and orienting frameworks of ethnographic research and provide a compelling entry point to some of the most urgent issues faced by people around the globe today.

Recent Books in the Series

Sugar: An Ethnographic Novel by Edward Narain and Tarryn Phillips (2024)

Bloom Spaces: Reproduction and Tourism on the Caribbean Coast of Costa Rica by Susan Frohlick (2024)

Under Pressure: Diamond Mining and Everyday Life in Northern Canada by Lindsay A. Bell (2023)

Fat in Four Cultures: A Global Ethnography of Weight by Cindi SturtzSreetharan, Alexandra Brewis, Jessica Hardin, Sarah Trainer, and Amber Wutich (2021)

Esperanza Speaks: Confronting a Century of Global Change in Rural Panama by Gloria Rudolf (2021)

The Living Inca Town: Tourist Encounters in the Peruvian Andes by Karoline Guelke (2021)

Collective Care: Indigenous Motherhood, Family, and HIV/AIDS by Pamela J. Downe (2021)

I Was Never Alone, or Oporniki: An Ethnographic Play on Disability in Russia by Cassandra Hartblay (2020)

Millennial Movements: Positive Social Change in Urban Costa Rica by Karen Stocker (2020)

From Water to Wine: Becoming Middle Class in Angola by Jess Auerbach (2020)

Deeply Rooted in the Present: Heritage, Memory, and Identity in Brazilian Quilombos by Mary Lorena Kenny (2018)

Long Night at the Vepsian Museum: The Forest Folk of Northern Russia and the Struggle for Cultural Survival by Veronica Davidov (2017)

Truth and Indignation: Canada's Truth and Reconciliation Commission on Indian Residential Schools, second edition, by Ronald Niezen (2017)

Merchants in the City of Art: Work, Identity, and Change in a Florentine Neighborhood by Anne Schiller (2016)

Ancestral Lines: The Maisin of Papua New Guinea and the Fate of the Rainforest, second edition, by John Barker (2016)

Love Stories: Language, Private Love, and Public Romance in Georgia by Paul Manning (2015)

Culturing Bioscience: A Case Study in the Anthropology of Science by Udo Krautwurst (2014)